Winston Churchill

and the Story of Two World Wars

Books by

OLIVIA COOLIDGE

Greek Myths

Legends of the North

The Trojan War

Egyptian Adventures

Cromwell's Head

Roman People

Winston Churchill
and the Story of Two World Wars

Winston Churchill

and the Story of

Two World Wars

OLIVIA COOLIDGE

Illustrated with photographs

HOUGHTON MIFFLIN COMPANY BOSTON

The Riverside Press Cambridge

We should like to credit the following sources for photographs that appear in the book: Bettman Archives for the photographs of Lady Randolph Churchill; Lord Randolph Churchill; and Churchill as a war correspondent. United Press International for the photographs bearing the following captions: First Lord of the Admiralty, World War I; The Atlantic Pact, 1941; "We shall let them have it back"; Costume for the Blitz; Former Naval Person; Big Three at Yalta; A splendid uniform; Electioneering; A green old age; Famous Victory sign; Churchill bows out; and Pomp and pageantry. Wide World Photos, Inc., for the photographs bearing the following captions: The Munich Crisis; That nice flying boat; On the bank of the Rhine; With friend and dog; Britain's highest honor; and Eighty-five today. Ben Roth Agency, Inc., for the PUNCH cartoon captioned A Student Pilot. The Imperial War Museum for the photographs captioned: At a forward observation post; and The Supreme Moment, V–E Day.

CONTENTS

"Arm yourselves and be ye men of valor, and be in readiness for the conflict; for it is better for us to perish than to look upon the outrage of our nation and our altar."

Quoted by WINSTON CHURCHILL *in his first broadcast to the British nation, May 19, 1940.*

Preface

THE LIFE OF CHURCHILL is the history of the first half of the twentieth century. Entering Parliament in 1901, he rose in the course of a very few years to a position in which every major event in England's affairs was part of his life story. Few men have ever hovered so long on the edge of supreme power and attained it so late. When at last he did, the future of the whole world was so bound up with England's that all appeared to depend on the capacity and the courage of this one man.

It is this that makes the life of Churchill difficult reading, yet fascinating to so many. No man in his lifetime can have had more books written on him than Churchill. To understand him, however, or even to cover the record of his achievements is not easy. His own books on the subject would fill a long shelf. Those who have ventured to compress his life into a single volume have either written for an English audience bred in English ways, or perhaps have tried to conceal their difficulties by a flow of anecdote, not always carefully checked. Yet this interplay of Churchill's life with history must be to those of our time its greatest value.

To say this is not to suggest that a life of Churchill should ever at any moment presume to be dull. He was never bored himself, for one thing. For another, people who knew him found him intensely stimulating. There was no limit to the range of his interests and the flow of his ideas, no limit either to his warm appreciation of courage and resource. Yet for all his brilliance, he was in some ways a very simple man. His wit, for instance, was singularly kindly, far more often enjoyable than sharp. He was a fighter in a frank, all-out style, who could say on hearing of Mussolini's end, "So the bloody beast is dead!" Yet there was no malice in him. Part of his charm, in fact, was his straightforward fashion of doing and saying what he felt with a fine heedlessness. It is this quality which made him drag his commander-in-chief down to the beach in Egypt to paddle and get wet. It accounts also for the endearing way in which he made himself unconsciously comic . . . witness the occasion when he went up onto the roof one winter's night to watch the Blitz, plumped down on the nearest half-seen object and sat there, assuring his attendants that, no, he was perfectly safe and beautifully warm . . . until unfortunates who had been at work in the office below came up to complain that they had been smoked out by the Prime Minister sitting square on the top of their chimney.

Greatness is a quality hard to analyze, a combination perhaps of character with achievement. At all events, it must be developed; it is not inborn. Churchill's native equipment included ability, determination, and courage; but the constant criticisms leveled at him in his earlier years were by no means frivolous. He really was rash, too eager for his own ideas, too much in a hurry. Bitter experience was needed to grind his qualities down to the point where they could be useful. The slow development of his true genius alone makes Churchill's life a remarkable study. Stronger even than this is the sense throughout that the man fits the age. Perhaps all great men have done so. Would Shakespeare, for instance, have become the genius we know if the current form of drama had been polite comedy? Could Shakespeare ever have developed his poetic gifts in such surroundings? Similarly, Churchill's qualities mark him out as the man for a supreme crisis. Had he carved out his career in Victorian England, he might have been remembered as a brilliant man; but would he have been called great? It seems unlikely.

Thus again and again through Churchill's life we are brought back to the study of his times. Without understanding these, we can only gape at Churchill in a meaningless way, accepting his appearance in the nick of time as we do some of the miracles of science. In actual truth, events had been preparing at an equal pace the moment and the man. They had chosen their candidate for greatness and had been shaping him for forty years. How they did so is neither his history nor theirs, but a blend of both.

Prologue

ON THE THIRTEENTH OF AUGUST, 1704, a battle was fought near the village of Blenheim by the Danube which changed the political balance of the world. Strangely enough, considering that it took place in Central Europe, its heroes were English. Europe was startled indeed, for it happened that the quality of English fighting men had been largely forgotten there since the days of Agincourt three centuries back. Nor had it seemed likely that England would produce a master of war who could beat the professionals of Europe at their own game. Yet as the last rays of the sun illuminated that stricken field with its thirty thousand dead and wounded men and its triumphant redcoats on guard over twelve thousand prisoners, it was clear the improbable thing had come to pass. The victor of Blenheim with a captive Marshal of France in his coach was seizing a moment to scribble a note to his wife on the back of an old tavern bill, assuring her that all was well with him and with the cause of England.

His name was John Churchill, and his present title, by favor of Queen Anne, was Duke of Marlborough. By origin he was in the social structure of those times a nobody. His father had been a respectable knight, Sir Winston Churchill, who had lost his modest fortune fighting for the King against the Parliament, and who had been compensated by odds and ends of pensions or jobs after the Restoration. One of these favors had been a place at court for young John and an army commission. Through the difficult intrigues of the next three reigns, John had risen to his present high position partly by luck, but very largely by remarkable abilities, not only as soldier, but as courtier and diplomat. At the moment of Blenheim, he was the first man in the kingdom, and his wife was the Queen's bosom friend. More striking yet, he was able to hold together a European coalition of a very motley sort. His brilliance actually dazzled German princelings into forgetting his birth. His patience persuaded Dutch merchants to whom caution was second nature that they dared trust their fortunes to his all-seeing competence. Even had he not been a soldier, John Churchill must have made his mark as a statesman.

It was Queen Anne's great good fortune to have had such a servant, for at the moment of her accession to the throne, the mighty struggle of King Louis XIV of France to dominate Europe was rising to its climax. The history of Europe since the sixteenth century has been a succession of such struggles. Each effort has been vaster than those preceding, and the effort of Louis came to be overshadowed in later times by that of Napoleon, of Wilhelm II, and of Hitler. Yet in his own day Louis was gigantic, and the genius who foiled him was by all standards of measurement as great a general as England ever produced.

No one has really understood why modest Sir Winston should have begotten such a son. Yet something there apparently was in Winston's blood, for his daughter's son became a Marshal of France. At all events, John Churchill himself was ambitious for his line and bequeathed his descendants the dukedom, the Palace of Blenheim built for him by a grateful queen, and one of the most splendid fortunes in Europe. Disappointingly, however, the Churchills did not amount to a great deal as the generations wore by. They had artistic tastes and spent their money on fine collections or on hobbies of a scientific sort. They were not stupid men, yet somehow or other they played no distinguished part.

Almost two hundred years went by since the Battle of Blenheim; and then unexpectedly the genius in the family flowered again. By now their actual kinship with Marlborough had by the mere passage of time become remote, yet Marlborough had left them besides a trace of his blood a living tradition. His gorgeous palace glowing with the memories of his glorious days provided a setting which might well fire an eager boy with noble ambition. And so in the course of centuries it came to pass.

JOHN WINSTON SPENCER CHURCHILL, seventh Duke of Marlborough, was in his day and age a perfect model of all a duke ought to be. Stern-looking, impressively framed in whiskers, sincerely religious, he was able enough to take active part in affairs of state, though without showing brilliance. He lived in style. The Queen's noblest subjects resided in Houses, Palaces, Courts, occasionally Castles. The Duke of Marlborough alone among his kind dwelt in a Palace, for Blenheim was far too splendid to be called anything else. Indeed, as a residence for a man without a particle of royal blood, it was unique in Europe. But then its founder, John, first Duke of Marlborough, had himself been unique. Thus, to the splendor of his mansion the seventh duke added the glory of being descended from an extraordinary man whose vast achievements had made their mark on Europe and on England. He also, naturally, was in possession of great wealth, although unhappily this was not as adequate as it had formerly been. However, he owned a priceless collection of jewels, of musical instruments, of engravings, Limoges enamels, rare books, four or five hundred paintings, and other treasures of such quantity and value that a cautious sale here and there for cash made little impression. John Winston, unlike almost every other

Duke of Marlborough, had no taste for the arts. He lived amid the collections of his ancestors without looking at them much, always conscious that Providence had placed him very high and would expect in return meticulous attention to his duty.

Like all men, the Duke had his troubles, some political and some domestic. In the summer of 1873 he received a letter from his younger and more promising son, Lord Randolph Churchill, which must have distressed him. Randolph wanted to marry. He had fallen head over heels in love with a girl and had got engaged to her after knowing her only three days. The Duke of Marlborough, who had been heir to a difficult father and now found himself father of a very difficult heir, had relied upon Randolph to uphold the honors of his name. The elder brother, the Marquis of Blandford, was already married to a suitable and beautiful girl with whom he had been much in love. Unfortunately, it turned out that the bride, though amiable, had not a brain in her head. The Marquis was already bored and would have caused various scandals if people had not been so kind in hushing them up. Small wonder that the Duke was skeptical now of the value of hot-headed love.

Besides, who was the girl? Randolph knew very little. Jennie Jerome was the second of three sisters who were at present residing with their mama in England. Papa, for reasons of business, lived in New York. This curious arrangement between a married pair cannot have pleased the Duke of Marlborough. And besides, one never quite knew who Americans were. It was true that a few years back, when the Empress Eugénie had been presiding over society in Paris, Mrs. Jerome and her daughters had been welcome in the very highest circles of all. But now that Emperor Napoleon III was dead, and the Empress Eugénie a refugee in England, people remembered that neither of them had really any background. Those who have risen from obscure positions themselves will receive wealthy strangers from nowhere at all. Eugénie's favor to the Jeromes was of course a recommendation, but of a modified sort. Who was this girl?

Inquiries produced one other unfortunate fact. There was not much money. Mr. Jerome had been very wealthy, but now, alas, he was not so. Randolph was destined to make a name for himself in Parliament and probably would never earn. He had money — he was bound to have some; but younger sons of dukes are never rich. Randolph would be moving all his life in a social group which he could not afford. It behooved him to marry the right sort of girl who was also an heiress.

A few of these reflections the Duke imparted to his son, though he restrained himself in a way which did him credit. He may have been startled when the Jeromes took immediate offense. They did not look on the younger son of a duke as a very great catch. In fact, they rather thought the condescension if any was on their side, considering Jennie's talents and her opportunities. Very promptly Mrs. Jerome removed her brood to Paris, where Randolph was desired not to follow. Who was this girl?

Jennie was the daughter of Leonard and Clarissa Jerome and through her mother was one-eighth Iroquois Indian.

Her father was of New England stock, but had been brought up on a farm in upper New York State, one of eight brothers who divided among themselves a set of widely different characteristics. Leonard was one of the restless ones, an adventurer born, a gambler, a flamboyant man whose interests developed into passions. He had started out in law, set up in Rochester, then bought a newspaper there. Pretty soon the *Rochester Daily American* had been developed into an outspoken Republican paper which was attracting fairly wide notice. All these stages in Leonard's career were preliminary, however, to the real business of his life, which only started in 1854 when he had scraped together enough to move to New York and go into business with his brother Addison on Wall Street.

In a few years, Leonard Jerome was a millionaire. The times were favorable, and his methods were new. After lavish entertaining and plenty of champagne, he would piece together gossip about the financial standing of this organization or that. When he was ready to strike, he gambled heavily on his knowledge and usually won. Meanwhile, his reputation as a spender mounted as gaily as his bank balance. Everything was done on a vast scale. When little Jennie wanted to skate in Central Park, he made a private ice rink for her instead. He then fitted up two cottages for the reception of guests, hired a band, and brought down three trainloads of friends to open it in style. His daughter's debut was celebrated by a banquet which cost ten thousand dollars and in which the center of the table was a pond thirty feet long with four live swans upon it and surrounded by a massive bank of flowers. At another huge party, champagne flowed from one fountain and Eau de Cologne from another.

In 1860, Jerome bought a quarter share in the *New York Times,* whose editorial policy he for a while controlled. He was an ardent supporter of Lincoln, and throughout the Civil War he managed to combine open-handed generosity to Northern causes with war profiteering on a truly magnificent scale. Everyone else did the same if he could, after all. Business went on as usual.

Meanwhile, Clarissa Jerome's toilettes grew more and more elaborate to match, but her expression was not contented. The world of finance and men's business luncheons was not for her. Clarissa always hankered after a society where women played a larger part. Not only did she have to remain in the background of her gay husband's success, but even his amusements were not hers. Leonard Jerome had two passions, horses and music. Clarissa shared neither. This did not deter him from enjoying himself in the least. The racecourse at Jerome Park and the American Jockey Club were his creations. His famous stables on Madison Square were of red brick faced with marble and decorated within by paneling, plate glass, and carpeted floors. Above the stables was a huge private theater in which the opera singer whom Leonard favored at the time might star with an amateur troupe.

It was the opera which caused most trouble. Clarissa had already put up with one budding genius in her home for over a year. She had listened with indulgence to her husband's raving over Jenny Lind, the Swedish Nightingale. She had even consented to call their second girl Jennie.

She had, however, no ear for music herself. Besides, as Leonard grew older he grew more extravagant in his gestures and caused talk. His magnificent present of a barouche with two white ponies to a young, but talented star embarrassed Clarissa. His private opera house was very much worse. The absolute climax was a "silver, gold, and diamond dinner" given to the star and her theatrical friends, Clarissa not being present. When Leonard got home after this particular orgy, his wife had made up her mind. She informed him that her health required her old family doctor, now practicing in Paris; while the girls' education was in need of a French finishing touch. There was no quarrel. Leonard was welcome to visit his wife in Europe. He was more than welcome to pay for her appearance with her daughters at the Imperial court, where the Empress Eugénie understood dress and set an expensive example. All the children were musical. Clarissa's own ear might be defective, but she understood the importance of female accomplishments. The best masters must certainly be secured. Clarissa never went back to New York, and the unfortunate Leonard found himself deprived of the daughters he adored and doomed to struggle with failing luck and tottering fortunes while the expenses of his family in Europe went on mounting.

Jennie, the second of these three sisters, was the dark one, and in the photographs at least the most attractive. Clara was the more beautiful, but Jennie had a twinkle. There was something independent in the carriage of her beautifully shaped little head, while the extreme darkness of her hair and eyes gave her character. Even as a girl she seems to have made an impression on much older people by the mixture of natural frankness with her beautifully trained party manners. The Misses Jerome's education had fitted them for the highest social spheres. They might have graced an embassy, or a dukedom, or the palace of a prince. None of them did. Here Jennie was throwing herself away on Lord Randolph Churchill, whom one certainly could not discourage, but who to Clarissa may have been a slight disappointment. What did Jennie see in him?

It was not with good looks that Jennie fell in love. Lord Randolph Churchill was rather a small and frail young man with a face more odd than handsome. At this time he had not developed the vast and drooping mustaches which later gave him a somewhat fishlike appearance when taken together with his large, protruding eyes. His present small mustache emphasized the tendency of his lower lip to stick out. His forehead was good, but too wide for his face in general, and thus not so much impressive as another oddity. His manner, however, had very great charm, and his conversation had wit. He brought to everything that he did a gaiety which had nothing to do with high spirits. It was rather a spark of electric tension which other people took for enjoyment, but which tired its possessor out. Indeed, he suffered from a sense of not caring very much about his life or prospects. His abilities were obviously great, but he did not yet feel certain that he really wanted to use them. The serious business of life had not yet gripped him, while immediate pleasures, such as riding for instance, were more vivid. Yet amid these latter he suffered from a feeling of waste and frustration . . . that is, he had done so until Jennie came into his life. With her by his side, so he assured his father ecstatically, the future would take on a different aspect.

The Duke of Marlborough exacted from his son a promise to wait six months and see; but correspondence and occasional visits to Paris could not be cut off. Randolph did not change his mind. The Duke, who had an affectionate nature, was clearly going to have to make the best of things if he valued relations with his son. Besides, an election was shortly due to take place, and Randolph stated that he would not stand for Parliament without being promised his Jennie . . . and an income sufficient to support her. The Duke must go over to Paris in order to meet his son's promised bride. The Duke did so, and was quite captivated. Leonard Jerome, now almost bankrupt, beggared himself to find a dowry. Randolph dutifully let himself be elected to Parliament. The wedding took place.

Randolph took his bride straight home to Blenheim. Later on, during the Season and at times when Parliament met, there would have to be a London house. Meanwhile, Blenheim was his home and his pride. It was big enough, moreover, to house a regiment besides the Duke and the Duchess, their three unmarried daughters, the Marquis of Blandford, and anyone else who might be visiting. In that generation, brides did not expect to be left alone with their husbands, and on the whole Jennie managed well. Randolph's unmarried sisters, less accomplished and less well dressed, were sometimes jealous, she thought. There was occasional awkwardness with the Duchess, who was a woman of exceptional strength of character, while Jennie herself had a mind of her own. The family life of the Marlboroughs was rather dull. Their dinners were dreadfully formal. In the evening, one might read a book or play whist. On the stroke of eleven, each member of the family lit his bedroom candle, kissed the Duke and Duchess good night, and went to bed. Luckily there was riding, shooting or hunting in season, and plenty of visiting. The Marquis of Blandford moved in a fashionable set, while Lord Randolph himself attracted friends. People of all ages came to stay, and Jennie entered into festivities with spirit. Indeed, she overdid it. For on the thirtieth of November, 1874, she was hastily hustled from a shooting party into the nearest downstairs room at Blenheim, which had to be cleared of ladies' wraps to receive her. There, in makeshift surroundings whose dinginess is an embarrassment to the owners of Blenheim today, Jennie gave birth to her first boy, a seven-months' baby, who was christened Winston Leonard Spencer Churchill in remembrance of ancestors on either side of the Atlantic.

In 1874, Lord Randolph had entered Parliament, he had married, he had had a son. The world was at his feet. He did nothing with it. He was too happy for ambition, too proud of his Jennie and her instant social success. With a star in her dark hair, she sailed through the London season, actually startling people with her combination of beauty and vigorous health. An evening without a ball was an evening wasted. Every night one went to bed at 5 A.M. Lord Randolph, whose constitution was far less strong than hers, must have lacked energy to pay more than routine attention to Parliament. He was no more attracted to the political scramble than ever, while his other pleasures had taken on new life with Jennie beside him.

This gay and superficial existence was interrupted by a famous social quarrel. The Marquis of Blandford and the Prince of Wales fell out about a lady. The Prince, whose conduct had been as reprehensible as Blandford's, took advantage of his position to pretend concern and outraged virtue. Lord Randolph, furious, threatened to publish indiscreet letters written by the Prince if he would not leave Blandford alone. As between gentlemen, Lord Randolph's support of his brother under such provocation seems excusable. The Prince, however, was not a gentleman, but the heir to the throne. One may not threaten Royalty, however much it may chance to have deserved it. The Prince gave notice that henceforward he would not enter a house in which Lord Randolph was received. Society conformed. Indeed, it really felt that Randolph had done an impossible thing. Poor Jennie's social success was suddenly over.

The bitterness caused by this ostracism made a new man of Randolph and turned his attention to the serious business of politics. His conversion was not immediate. Indeed, for four years after this he was little in London. It was not till 1880 that Lord and Lady Randolph made their second bid to conquer the world, this time in the circles where speeches were made, where ladies went canvassing for their husbands, where entertainments were frequently talks with national figures, and where the cartoonists seized on Randolph's mustaches with joy, while the reporters made capital out of his wit. "Randy Pandy" was a sensation from the first, and in a few years was a national figure.

British political life in Victorian times was dominated by two parties, Liberal and Conservative, whose names more or less represented their political programs. In 1880, the Liberals had a majority in the Commons and according to the British system "formed a government." In other words, they chose from among themselves all the executive officers of state. Chief among these was the extraordinary figure of Mr. Gladstone, whose magnificent appearance, keen mind, and earnest character had made him the most re-markable politician of the reign. Gladstone was now sev-enty-one and Prime Minister for the second time. His pre-vious administration had been one of the most brilliant of the century and had earned him an admiration which was quite irrespective of party. The Conservative opposition might detest him, but they were awed. In 1880, they rather inclined to say nothing much and to hope that his powers would fail soon. They underestimated his physique, as it happened. Gladstone was to be Prime Minister once more at eighty-three.

The Conservative Party, in a minority at this time, was leaderless, or nearly so. The brilliant Disraeli was old and ailing. He had lately taken a peerage and a seat in the House of Lords as semi-retirement. He was not, however, dead; and there were two possible claimants for the leader-ship when vacant. The abler of these, Lord Salisbury, was a hereditary peer and sat in the House of Lords. It was not impossible then, as it is now, to govern England from the Lords; but it was felt to be a drawback, especially as Salis-bury was no successful politician who had been promoted, but a man whose whole political life had been lived up there. He had never, for instance, fought an election. He had never crossed swords with Mr. Gladstone. Could he do so if he tried? The other leader, Sir Stafford Northcote, sat in the Commons; but as for crossing swords with Mr. Gladstone, it was quite clear that he could not. He did not attempt it, and his party under his influence sat mute.

Lord Randolph Churchill was the exception to this rule. He had no awe of Gladstone, and he set himself to bait the great man in every fashion which a lively wit could suggest. He would ask him a question. Gladstone, who was a great man for facts and a terrible talker, would answer at length. Randolph would smile blandly and ask him another. Presently the House would get restive and everybody but Gladstone would have a suspicion that Randolph was amused. Randolph's interruptions were terrible, too. They were funny, outrageous, and as rude as the rules of the Commons would allow. His speeches tore Gladstone to shreds, depicting his earnestness as priggish hypocrisy, dismissing his popular appeal as propaganda. Randolph had real talent for speaking, and some of the phrases he used were apt to stick. Presently the general public began to find this duel between the grand old man and the irrepressible young one entertaining. Cartoonists took it up. The name of Lord Randolph became a household word.

It was only natural that the contrast between Lord Randolph's behavior and that of his party leaders should have caused ill-feeling between them. Disraeli had been amused, but he had died. Sir Stafford Northcote, who felt his tactics challenged, was annoyed. Lord Randolph in his turn despised Sir Stafford and the big men of the party. In fact, he called them the Goats, and that name stuck. He was making enemies inside his own ranks as well as outside them. For Lord Randolph had a policy for the Conservative Party for which he had also coined a name. He wanted them to adopt what he called "Tory Democracy."

The British electorate until within recent years had more or less consisted of those who owned the houses they lived in. The working classes living in lodgings and the agricultural laborers living in cottages on the estate had no vote. This was now changed. The size of the electorate had been very greatly increased, and all the new voters were the poorer, more ignorant members of the community. The propertied classes of the Conservative Party, who liked things as they were, seemed inclined to hope that these groups would feel their dependence on trade and their employers, and that they would be nervous of change. Lord Randolph Churchill perceived that in the long run this would not be so. The Conservative Party must take a new line and appeal to the people with a program of social reform. It must show them that the interests of all were bound up together. The poorer classes could travel farther by co-operation with those in power than by class strife, since the prosperity of the nation must profit all.

Lord Randolph began to appeal to the people himself. He started speaking all over the country, using his resources of nervous energy to great effect. He acted against his own leaders directly and forced them to hand over the management of the party funds to an elected committee. Meanwhile, the death of Disraeli was felt all over the country as the passing of a remarkable man. His favorite flower had been the primrose. Everyone was wearing a primrose stuck in his lapel.

Randolph and some friends had a brilliant idea. Why not develop the wearers of the primrose into a league? The intention of the Primrose League was to provide a place inside the Conservative Party where the upper class and the workingman could really rub elbows. Its chief business was to hold fetes out of doors. There would be a short political speech, not too tedious, then sports and refreshments. Everybody would mingle with everybody else, while the ladies, though voteless, would be as important as the men. This simple form of political get-together proved surprisingly effective. It was true that the working classes had little chance in general to meet with their betters. Their lives, too, were tediously dull, and any entertainment was welcome. Witness the popularity of Randolph himself. He was always good entertainment.

It had now become obvious that inside the Conservative Party Lord Randolph was the coming man. The Goats were afraid of him or distrusted him, but they could not do without his popular reputation. Every day at Harrow School when the roll was called outside in the yard, a little crowd gathered to see Lord Randolph's redheaded son answer to his name. As they did so, some tactless soul would remark quite audibly, "Why, he's the last boy in school!" Lord Randolph was coming to the conclusion that Winston must be stupid. He did not seem so; yet school reports said he was. It was not too difficult for a boy of average ability to learn Latin, given time; yet Winston could not. In the next generation, Lord Randolph would have changed his son's school. In this one, there was only one type of education which all boys must fit. Winston somehow never could do it.

Humiliated by a lack of success which he himself did not understand, Winston drank in his father's. He had little time in which to do so, for that brilliant career was incredibly short. In 1886, the Conservatives took office. Lord Salisbury, thanks to Lord Randolph's aid, had won out over Sir Stafford. He became Prime Minister. Randolph was Chancellor of the Exchequer, second executive officer of state, and leader of the government party in the House of Commons. He was only thirty-seven and the youngest Chancellor in a hundred years. There seemed no limit to what he might become if his health held out.

Unluckily it soon turned out that Lord Randolph's position was not so secure as it seemed or as he fancied. Lord Salisbury did not trust him, nor did the Cabinet as a whole believe in Tory Democracy. Lord Randolph, like many a sensible man, belonged somewhere in the middle between the two great parties. When therefore in 1886 he tried to drive the Conservative leaders into social reform, he was really imposing a Liberal policy which they resented.

Schemes of reform cost money. As Chancellor, it was Lord Randolph's duty to provide the sums needed. He planned to do so partly by taxation, partly by economies, among which he demanded naval and military cutbacks. The Admiralty was brought to consent, but the Minister of War, Mr. Smith, was made of sterner stuff. He had also been the target of some sharp remarks by Lord Randolph in debate which the press had thought very funny. For whatever reason, Mr. Smith refused to reduce his estimates, and he accused Lord Randolph of trying to bully the whole government into doing what he personally wanted. Lord Salisbury played umpire as long as he could, then backed Mr. Smith. The sum in question was not really very large, and a wiser man than Randolph might have put up with the loss. But Randolph had made his reputation by never refusing a fight. Besides, he was overworked and his nerves were not good. Lord Randolph resigned.

He did it at the worst possible time and in the worst possible way. He was actually staying with the Queen, and he wrote his resignation to Lord Salisbury on Palace stationery. Thus Victoria was deeply insulted at not having been considered or told. Meanwhile Lord Salisbury, who understood perfectly well that Lord Randolph was trying to pull the government down if he did not get his way, was looking around for new friends and found some. Contrary to expectation, he was able to carry on the government without Lord Randolph. The meteor had blazed across the skies and gone out. The race was ended.

Lord Randolph did not accept the fact that he was finished, and the public did not understand it. He plunged back into the fray with his usual vigor. Before long, however, it was not Mr. Gladstone or even the Goats with whom he found himself locked in struggle, but with Death.

Lord Randolph's health had never been good, and any period of intense activity had always had to be followed by vacation and rest. Eventually his symptoms of numbness in the hands or feet and occasional clumsiness became alarming. The doctors diagnosed a progressive paralysis of the entire system, incurable and only to be delayed somewhat by taking things easy. Lord Randolph merely kept his condition a secret and worked himself into minor breakdowns, after which Jennie would have to take him abroad. Here people, aware of his great reputation and not up to date on English news, received him with honor. The English papers, which had once hung on his every word, now omitted a few — then omitted paragraphs — then skated over his speech in a sentence or two. Randolph's articulation was affected. It became a real struggle to get words out clearly. His brilliant mind slowed down, seemed almost confused.

Jennie worked for him like a Trojan. She canvassed at elections, took a prominent part in the Primrose League, knew everyone intimately, and pulled every wire worth pulling. Randolph's mother, the Dowager Duchess, did the same. But Randolph grew worse and worse, yet would not admit it; and nothing went right. Young Winston was still a dunce in school. No one took enough notice of his remarkable memory or his power with words, for if a boy could not master Latin grammar, he must be something of a fool.

Randolph was proud of the boy's manliness, but distant with him as Victorian fathers were apt to be. The two could not talk. It had been decided that Winston should enter the army, since the university was clearly going to be impossible, and he must earn. But there were army examinations in English, mathematics, French, and Latin.

Latin was hopeless, and French not much less so. Winston's articulation was defective, and he lisped. This may have been a reason why modern languages, though easier than Latin to him, were more or less barred. It was necessary for him to pass in two subjects in order to enter the army. Mathematics was a complete muddle to him and always had been. He now went firmly back to the beginning and in six months had mastered the subject. Nobody noticed that this achievement was far more uncommon than learning mathematics from the start like the average boy. Randolph merely perceived that his son was too low on the Army list to get into the infantry, while the cavalry — what with their uniforms and horse — always needed money beyond what they earned. He was angry and disappointed, the more so because he knew well he had little to leave. He did not foresee that plenty of riding and sensible studies like tactics would make up the change in education of which his remarkable son stood so much in need. For the first time in his life, Winston was not going to be bored by learning. Moreover, he was going to be a success. Nobody ever for an instant was going to imagine that Winston was stupid again.

Randolph, however, was bitterly depressed. Even he could perceive in the end that his struggle was hopeless. He wanted no sympathy and rejected even his son's. His health grew worse. Someone, droning away in the House of Commons, happened to mention by way of an illustration St. Peter and St. Paul. Quite suddenly Randolph burst out, "The Apostle Paul!" His strange, slurring accents and the absolute nonsense of making such a correction drew all eyes. It was clear that Lord Randolph no longer knew what was going on, and his appearance was that of a dying man. His mortal illness could no longer be concealed. He was helped home, and this time Jennie took him on a voyage round the world, on which for a while he grew better. At Canton, they ran into a riot and were almost mobbed. Randolph stopped his palanquin in front of a jeweler's shop, got out, deliberately pushed aside the howling throng, and bought a green jade bracelet. As he offered it to Jennie, he said, "To remember me." Then realizing he had given himself away, he made a hasty correction, "To remember this day." It was one of his last typical acts. When Jennie brought him home, he was a mere shadow of himself, hardly able to speak or understand. Winston was twenty, and his life was about to begin. His brother Jack was fourteen. Poor Jennie, a little stouter now, but still a beauty, after Jack was finally launched, married again. At the end of her varied life, however, she was buried next to Randolph where she belonged, just outside Blenheim.

It took a war to make Winston Churchill famous. This was not a great war as modern wars go, nor was it a glorious one. The British, who have many wars in their history, prefer to skate over the Boer War of 1899 to 1902 without dwelling on details. Other nations are apt to speak of it as a war of aggression in which a powerful, imperialistic England swallowed up two gallant little South African republics who defended themselves for several years with extraordinary skill. This verdict, though certainly true in part, is not quite fair. The chief cause of the Boer War was the discovery of gold in the Boer republic of Transvaal, which attracted foreign capital and foreign immigrants in such large numbers that the life of its network of simple Dutch farming communities was seriously threatened. The Boers protected themselves by taxing foreign industry very sharply without allowing the aliens who owned it any rights. This policy was in contradiction to earlier treaties and bred quarrels which were taken up by the British South African colonies surrounding the Boer republics. The British government, internally divided, put pressure on the Boers, yet made no preparations for war. The Boers for their part began in the early nineties to spend their tax money on quantities of modern weapons, mainly German. The neighboring colonies, alarmed by this, appealed to Great Britain, who finally decided to send a garrison force into her South African possessions. Taking this as a direct threat, the Boers invaded. Their action unified Great Britain as a whole, yet throughout the country, and even in Parliament, a small minority held out against the war. This did not, naturally, include young Winston Churchill, who had spent his twenty-first birthday — in his own free time and at his own expense — under fire in Cuba, and who had in the next four years taken in two small wars and narrowly missed a third, owing to resistance from people higher up, who thought him a nuisance.

The invasion by the Boers was not pure rashness. What they hoped for was a series of early successes, followed by a rising of the many Dutch farmers in Cape Colony, by the aid of whom they might just possibly sweep the English back to the sea. The German emperor, who had already shown some sympathy, might intervene. Other countries looked sourly on Great Britain for various reasons. At all events, the Boers were by now ready for war, and by invading at well-selected spots, they attracted South African forces into difficult terrain. In no direction was strategy of this kind more likely to bring them profit than eastward in Natal.

Natal lies on the east coast of South Africa and consists in general of a wide coastal plain which narrows farther inland into a tongue of land twisting up between hills as far as the border of the Transvaal. This tongue of land was not defensible against a well-mounted, well-disciplined invading force. Its little townships sat in valleys almost surrounded by rolling foothills from which they could be commanded. The railroad running up from Durban on the coast was very easy to cut in numerous places, yet as the defendants fell back, the invading army could bring up its own supplies out of Johannesburg along it. The key to this whole tongue of land, and therefore to Natal, was Ladysmith, strategically as difficult to hold as anywhere else, but a junction of the railroads running to the coast out of the Transvaal and out of the other republic, the Orange Free State. It might have been wiser for General Sir George White, commander of the forces which Natal had hastily brought up for defense, to evacuate Ladysmith and fall back while he had time. But Sir George was subject to pressure from the outraged farmers of Natal, and he was conscious that behind him no defense works had been put in hand. There were, moreover, considerable stores in Ladysmith which he did not want to lose. The consequence was that he lingered and was very shortly cut off inside the town with the only army which Natal then could boast, since British reinforcements had not yet appeared.

In the face of this crushing disaster, there was little to be done. At Pietermaritzburg, seventy miles behind the line, earth fortifications were being hastily thrown up under someone's direction. At Durban, fifty miles farther back, they were installing naval guns. What passed for a front line was now established at Estcourt, a railroad town of about three hundred houses, mostly of corrugated iron, some thirty miles from Ladysmith. Here Colonel Wolfe Murray was rather nervously awaiting a further advance of the Boer army with all the men he could collect. His forces amounted to about two thousand in all, most of them regular soldiers, but the rest consisting of Natal volunteers, mounted police, a band of cyclists, a battery of nine-pounder guns, a very small armored train, and the war correspondent of the *Morning Post,* Mr. Winston Churchill, almost twenty-five years old and enjoying every minute as it came.

Estcourt, though quite a considerable town as towns there went, was not strategically any stronger than Ladysmith had been, while the forces holding it were just one-fifth as large. Colonel Murray was anxious to look imposing, of course; but his chief anxiety was to know when the Boers were coming in time to fall farther back. The siege of Ladysmith was delaying them for a while, but it seemed probable they would leave a force behind to deal with that and press on very soon. Accordingly, the Colonel sent out his mounted police and his cyclists and so forth to reconnoiter the country as close to Ladysmith as they dared; and since he had it, he thought he might as well use the armored train.

The armored train was an unimpressive object with a few bullet-proof trucks and a little engine which ran for some reason in the middle. However, it was transport; and Colonel Murray, whose total mobile forces did not amount to over three hundred men, was duly grateful for anything that he could get. So also was Mr. Churchill, who had with his usual enterprise managed to find a berth on the boat which was bringing out from England the new commander-in-chief. He had left this worthy in Cape Town, and by an adventurous dash over threatened railroads he had arrived at the Natal front far in advance of other reinforcements, but without the chance to collect a horse or even a bicycle. He was therefore compelled to reconnoiter by armored train or sit in Estcourt. Naturally the fact that the soldiers spoke of their train as a "death trap" did not deter him in the least. Thus the armored train was sent chugging very slowly up the line in search of news with a company of soldiers, a breakdown gang, an old-fashioned, muzzle-loading popgun, and Mr. Churchill with a pair of binoculars and a pistol just in case. Every few miles it panted into a station with a clump of trees and a half-dozen tin houses, now deserted save by a few scrounging natives with whom it might confer. If it came to a bridge or a culvert, the breakdown men would have to get out and look this over in case the Boers had sent out a raiding party to damage the line. Meanwhile, men could search the horizon with their binoculars, or even focus on the distant dot of the Ladysmith balloon, which Boer artillery was unable to shoot down, and which hung over the besieged, invisible town like a flag of defiance. Having thus crept up toward the enemy as far as it dared and seen nothing much, the train could go home to report that for another day the enemy had not advanced.

This was all very well, but within a week of Churchill's arrival, the Boers did advance, and what is more they ambushed the train. Having frightened it into starting home in a hurry, they opened fire on it with artillery after carefully placing a large stone just round a bend in the middle of the line. What with the resulting crash and the artillery fire and the Boer rifles, which had by now joined in, there were many wounded and great confusion followed. Winston Churchill, according to the general impression, was everywhere at once and took command. The engine driver, who was a civilian and who had been hurt, seemed ready to quit. He appears to have been given the notion in a hectic interview under fire that nobody ever was wounded twice on the same day and that there certainly would be a medal for him . . . as there was many years later when Churchill had some influence in these affairs. Somehow the engine was disentangled from the wreck under Churchill's orders. Forty wounded were packed onto the tender. The rest of the soldiers were ordered to scramble up the line, sheltering from enemy fire behind the engine as it moved. This proved, however, to be impossible. The unwounded soldiers were speedily left behind and forced to surrender. Winston Churchill, who had started out on the tender to keep control of the affair, slipped off it and ran back to rally his men. He only succeeded in being chased for his life and taken prisoner by a Boer called Louis Botha, who later became first president of the Union of South Africa and a personal friend.

Meanwhile the armored train, what was left of it, went back to Estcourt with its forty wounded aboard and reported the Boers coming on. The soldiers attributed their escape to the gallant efforts of Winston Churchill. Very naturally, the *Morning Post,* which was London's most powerful Conservative daily, gave plenty of space to the exploits of its correspondent. Everybody in town who was anybody knew about Winston Churchill, who was connected by blood with numerous members of the House of

Lords and known to the House of Commons as the son of a famous father not long dead. Thus his capture created quite a stir. Regrets and fears for his safety were widely expressed. None of this, however, made a hundredth part of the sensation caused by his escape from Pretoria some weeks later.

The name of Lord Randolph Churchill was not unknown in South Africa, and it had only taken the Boers a few hours to discover whose son their prisoner was. They were pleased with themselves and for that reason all the more angry when Churchill disappeared after a short incarceration in the State Model School in Pretoria, which had been fitted up as an officers' prison. They promptly circulated their loss far and wide, no doubt expecting to catch him very soon. Their unflattering description gives a reasonable picture of Churchill's appearance at this time.

"Wanted: Englishman twenty-five years old; about five feet eight inches tall, of indifferent build; walks with a slight stoop; pale appearance, red-brown hair, small mustache hardly perceptible; talks through the nose, cannot pronounce 's' properly and does not know any Dutch."

They might have added that he was a young man of exceptional audacity, never at a loss for a good idea and always fortunate in the matter of hairbreadth escapes. No doubt they did not know that much and only learned it when Churchill clambered out of a train in Lourenço Marques, a Portuguese East African port into which he had been smuggled under bales of goods exported from the Transvaal.

Meanwhile, in England, the papers had expressed surprise at Churchill's escape without much expectation that he would be long at large. The Boers reported him recaptured here or there, and then denied it. Ten days passed. The war, which had begun badly for England, was now going worse. The British army had not fought a civilized foe for fifty years. It now appeared that their weapons were quite inferior to German ones, while their commanders were worse than inexperienced. The slow promotions and the tiny army of peacetime had played a part in keeping able men out of military life. Tidings of disaster were published day after day to a population both puzzled and appalled. Could no one do anything right? Was the vast power of England actually unequal to a struggle with Dutch farmers? Mr. Winston Churchill's spirited escape was felt to be the sort of gesture which someone ought to make, yet naturally nothing would come of it. Nothing ever did these days. Happily this time the public turned out to be wrong, and Churchill got clean away.

The British consulate at Lourenço Marques was used to down-and-outs very likely, people who clamored to see the consul personally and wanted him summoned from his bath, his meal, or his bed for some purpose which they did not wish to declare, but which undoubtedly boiled down to asking for money. A filthy young man with a sprouting red beard was nothing new. The consul's secretary was not impressed. The consul, however, happened to look out of a window himself while the altercation went on and on. The young man outside announced his name. From that very moment, Churchill was a national hero. News spread like wildfire in the British community of the town. Everything was at his disposal. Eight or nine people with pistols gathered to form a guard, lest enterprising Boers should redeem their country's loss of face by kidnaping. Churchill was escorted aboard a British ship in harbor which was sailing by great good luck for Durban.

News had preceded him thither. A crowd awaited him. Amid cheers, a speech was demanded. Winston Churchill, who was not troubled by shyness, began to enjoy himself to such an extent that presently various people in England who had known him as a cavalry subaltern and thought him brash put their money together to send him a cable. "Best friends here hope you will not continue making further ass of yourself." It was too late, and they mistook their man. Young Churchill expressed himself without inhibitions now as always.

All the same, one can see their point of view. No doubt it had been annoying that such a very young man should cable his opinions to the *Morning Post* to the effect that one armed Boer was equal to four or five British soldiers. He had added further that an army of a quarter of a million would be needed. Experienced people could hardly be expected to see that he was right. They merely remembered that he had spent only four short years in the army and had seen a little service in India. There he had wangled his way into a frontier campaign on which he had written a book, undoubtedly vivid if one liked that sort of thing, but far too free in its judgments for such a very junior officer. Instead of returning to his regiment where he belonged for a few useful years of routine, he had made himself a nuisance pulling wires and trying to get posted to this trouble spot or to that. Being finally successful in attending part of the conquest of the Sudan against the wishes of the commanding general, he had written a still more ambitious book in which he criticized the general's personality none too politely. Now here he was again, and only twenty-five! He had actually added that irregular cavalry were needed and cabled the query, "Are the gentlemen of England all foxhunting?" He was outrageous. From the beginning, Winston's popularity was counterbalanced by his power of giving offense. People had no notion why a lucky escape from the Boers should qualify him to tell others their job.

They were not unreasonable, yet looking backward over Churchill's great career, one perceives a real fitness in the fact that his reputation was made in war. For Churchill possessed a genius for war. Had his life been otherwise, he might or he might not have made a great commander. As it was, war presented him with a challenge to which he responded with the fullest use of his faculties. In August, 1914, when civilization hung over the brink of the First World War, Mr. Asquith, then Prime Minister of Great Britain, commented on Winston's high spirits and thought him insensitive. No one who reads Winston's own account of those days can consider his feelings any less acute than Asquith's were. Indeed, in a way they were more so, since his imagination was more vivid. But whereas Asquith was appalled, Churchill rose to meet the occasion for which he was born, just as on a later and greater occasion he rose once more.

Meanwhile, in 1899 the excitement over young Churchill died down to some extent. Other people escaped from the

Boers with equal daring, but their adventures came after a favorable turn in the war and were less noticed. Churchill made no move to come home or cash in on his popularity there. He joined a South African corps of Light Horse and served in the bitter campaign in which the British fought their way back up to Ladysmith for two more months, and finally relieved it. His dispatches, however, went on coming out in the *Morning Post* and still caused annoyance. He was actually appealing for decent treatment of conquered enemies, while his acid comments on a sermon preached to the troops before battle offended Church of England dignitaries who might hitherto have ignored him. However, his position in South Africa was assured, and when at the end of the Ladysmith campaign he was anxious to transfer to the far more exciting invasion of the Boer republics by Lord Roberts, he succeeded. He and his cousin, the Duke of Marlborough, were therefore in a position to canter alone into Pretoria when it was known that the Boers had started to evacuate the town. They did so without waiting for the enemy to get out and found themselves facing the fifty-two guards of the State Model School with rifles ready. Marlborough called on these to surrender, and luckily they did. In another moment, the gates were open, prisoners were rushing out, someone produced a Union Jack, and the crisis was over.

The war was over too, as far as Churchill was concerned. It now degenerated into long guerrilla campaigns in which farmhouses were burned and women and children involved as much as men. Decencies were preserved to a surprising extent, yet nothing can make such a struggle otherwise than sordid and grim. It was time for young Churchill to pull more wires and go home. He had ambitions to enter Parliament, and had in fact stood for election just before the war without success. The way was now open, and he felt it his duty to press for a generous peace.

All went very well. The young hero carried the election and started out right away on a two-and-a-half month lecture tour through England and the United States in order to make his war experiences earn the money he would need for his support as an unpaid statesman. By the middle of February, 1901, he had been speaking six days a week for almost five months, and often twice a day. His fortune, however, was in the bank; his health had been equal to the strain; and Parliament was about to re-assemble. Lord Randolph Churchill's son with few opinions of his own on policy yet, but with an impressive capacity for work and an assurance very much strengthened by success made his formal entry. He felt on top of the world. He had arrived at twenty-six. Meanwhile, his excitement was not shared by the House of Commons, whose attention had been diverted by an almost equally important event. For in January of 1901, the end of a great era was reached. Queen Victoria died.

AGADIR was only a tiny Moorish town on the coast of Morocco which most people in 1910 had never heard of. True, it had a better natural harbor than Casablanca slightly farther north, and it was the outlet for a hinterland which promised to be fertile. But many years ago through local jealousies the port had been closed by the Sultan, since when it had moldered away and now consisted only of a fishing village with a few mud houses, goats, and dirt. No Europeans were allowed to live in it; and presumably few wanted to, or the nations who were now interested in Morocco might have put some pressure on the bankrupt Sultan to declare it open. They had not done this, and Agadir decayed at its own pace in the bright sun.

It may seem strange that Germany, France, and England should have hovered on the brink of war over Agadir in 1911, but such was the fact. It was hardly a question of wanting the miserable town, but rather of wondering what might be made of it by someone else. The French, who owned Algeria, were also predominant in Morocco. Now that the rule of the Sultan had collapsed into anarchy there, they were preparing to take over, protect European traders, and keep order. The British had agreed in return for a free hand in Egypt. Germany, however, who ranked third in Moroccan trade, had received no compensation for loss of her influence there, and she now felt free to demand some. Looking around, therefore, for a way to make their claim stick, the German Kaiser and his chancellor in an evil hour decided on a timely show of force. They sent a warship to take possession of the port of Agadir.

The *Panther* was a fairly small warship, and if the other nations had been perfectly sure what the Emperor intended, they might have remained calm. But then they never were. Kaiser Wilhelm II had succeeded unexpectedly to the Empire of Germany in 1888 when he was thirty. His sudden elevation was thought to have gone to his head. Now, over twenty years later, his neighbors in Europe were still not quite sure he had ever grown up. In actual fact, Wilhelm was a well-meaning man and not unintelligent; but he had the misfortune to have inherited a position to which he was not equal. Under the direction of ministers of his choosing, German diplomacy had moved from one threat of war to another, making enemies for the purpose of gaining small advantages. Emperor Wilhelm was afraid his people might think he was afraid of war, as indeed he quite sensibly was. His ministers were afraid of being thought unworthy of Bismarck, that iron Chancellor who had threatened wars, and fought them, and won, and unified the Germans. Accordingly they had threatened France with war in 1905, causing her to back down and immediately start to strengthen her army. They had threatened Russia in 1908, forcing her also to give way in a hurry and start to build up her military railroads. Now England in her turn was not sure if she were not as much of a target as France. For Agadir might easily be made into a naval station whose location would threaten British trade routes from South America, South Africa, and Suez. On the whole, Britain thought she had better ask German intentions.

The German Chancellor, pleased at having so clearly made an impression, returned no answer to England. Actually he preferred not to fight with England, but he was ready to go all lengths in bullying France. Accordingly he demanded in return for giving up German interest in Morocco the whole of French Equatorial Africa. No French statesman could have consented to such an outrageous price without betraying a willingness to let France sink to a second-class power and lose the confidence of her allies. Yet Germany as a neighbor in Morocco was not to be thought of.

English statesmen, brooding over the ominous silence of Germany, came to the conclusion that she did want to pick a quarrel with France, and possibly with England. They asked each other why if Germany did not want a war she went on arming. And in especial, why was she building up a fleet? British naval designers had some years back produced the superbattleship, the dreadnought, which could blow all other ships out of the water. As a result, almost overnight the British navy was suddenly obsolete. Any other great nation who wanted to start building dreadnoughts could more or less do so on a level with England. Germany had leaped at the chance. Nor could the British understand why, unless it were for aggression. Britain's navy was known to be essential to her life, which depended on sea-borne trade. Germany had little seacoast, no colonies of importance, and the strongest army in Europe. It stood to British reason that she could not be allowed the strongest fleet.

These calculations of the British mind were much discounted in Germany by the fact that they did not believe that the present British government wanted to fight. It was Liberal and contained some of the most brilliant political minds England had seen, but for that very reason it was deeply involved in a typically Liberal program of social and constitutional change. No one could have described Mr. Asquith, the Prime Minister, as warlike. His second-in-command, David Lloyd George, was a fiery little Welshman who had risen from complete obscurity and really understood the problems of the poor. He was absorbed by internal questions, had been against the Boer War from the beginning right through to the end, and was apt to dismiss international complications as expensive luxuries. The other member of the government much in the news was Winston Churchill, Home Secretary at this time, very much a disciple of the brilliant Lloyd George, who was ten years older. Winston, moreover, looked on himself as political heir to Lord Randolph Churchill, who had fallen from power while trying to enforce reduction in military expenses.

What the German statesmen did not foresee was that both Winston and Lloyd George himself were politically young and capable of learning. In this time of great anxiety, they both discovered that alarmist talk about Germany was not after all just nonsense. Germany was steadily putting herself in a position to have a war when she liked.

They rather imagined that if she could be sure England would stand out, she might fall on France at once. In fact, Lloyd George now thought it wiser to warn the Germans that England could not afford to see France beaten and then be tackled later. There is no better proof of the intensity of the Agadir war scare than the conversion of Lloyd George in the face of his upbringing, his interests, his desires, and his ambitions.

For the future of England, however, Churchill's convictions were more significant than Lloyd George's. Somewhat taken aback by the determination of England, Germany did finally consent to negotiations. But whereas Lloyd George at once turned back to the things he cared about, Winston Churchill for the first time in his political life started out on his own. The previous ten years of his career, fruitful though they had been, had merely formed a preliminary stage in his development as a statesman. We owe it to the Chancellor, the nationalist German press, and perhaps to Wilhelm II that Churchill found himself over the question of Agadir.

Lord Randolph's son had been welcomed into Parliament in 1901 by the Conservative Party, still under the leadership of Lord Salisbury and his nephew, Mr. Balfour. Nice things were said and felt since all past awkwardness might fairly be considered done and over. However, in a year or two when the Party had had leisure to sum young Winston up, its general impression was not too favorable. In the first place, Winston Churchill was by no means the accomplished orator that his father had been. He never did learn to manage the letter s, and his delivery suffered from a hesitation which at awkward moments was almost a stammer. His violent efforts to get his sentences out gave an effect of harshness which made him appear to be overexcited. Nor could he then speak from notes. It was for years his practice to write his speech out beforehand and learn it by heart. This had worked well on a lecture platform, but it now meant he could not adapt himself to the arguments of debate, while any emotion he might display seemed forced. Parliament, however, is used to all sorts of speakers, and it noted that Winston's speeches, though not yet well delivered, were uncommonly well expressed. The trouble about them was that he always seemed to be attacking his own party.

It is fair to say that the nature of the British government demands a rigid party system. Since all the officers of state are actually members of the dominant party in Parliament, it follows that when the balance of power is upset in the House of Commons, the government must be changed. If every member of the party in power felt free to criticize on points of policy he did not very much like, no British government would last long enough to get anything done. The individual member may be consulted by his leaders in private, but in the House he is expected to back his party up. Thus when it is in power he mostly has to sit silent while those who have done the detailed work explain their plans. In opposition, on the other hand, he may criticize freely. Lord Randolph Churchill had made his reputation very largely in opposition, but when Winston appeared upon the scene, his party was in power.

This situation, awkward enough at any time to an im-

patient man, was made much worse by the fact that the
Boer War was a subject on which young Churchill felt a
right to speak. This had been a Conservative war. A few
of the Liberals under Lloyd George opposed it utterly, while
the rest took the view that it might have been avoided
and should have been differently run. Many Conservatives,
on the other hand, had reacted with violent patriotism
and were talking loudly of reprisals. Churchill, who had
the generous view of the fighting man, was of the opinion
that mild and statesmanlike terms should be published at
once.

Some latitude is allowed. The Conservatives listened to
their youngest recruit on the South African question with
a certain tolerance. They did not, however, care for hearing Lord Randolph's opinions on a reduction in armaments
dished up at a moment when the Boer War had revealed
great military weakness. Moreover, fortified by the support
of the Primrose League throughout the country, they felt
no need for a further dose of Tory Democracy, which
had always seemed to them suspiciously Liberal. Churchill
found himself more and more on his feet and less and less
in harmony with the party.

Party loyalties are not changed lightly, and the enmities
aroused by doing so go very deep. Every so often, however,
party leaders will change direction on some fundamental
issue which excuses the rank and file from following
blindly. Luckily for Churchill, such a situation now arose.

In our age of managed economies, it is difficult to
imagine how sacred to both parties was the doctrine of
Free Trade. It was almost the one thing on which they

agreed. When other nations made a good thing out of tariffs, they were merely considered shortsighted and unable to take a world-wide view. But by 1900, British trade was feeling the wind of competition keenly. It was only a question of time before uncomfortable facts would force one party or the other into suggesting new remedies. That time now arrived for the Conservatives. Winston Churchill was unable to change his principles to suit. He said so loudly and often, until Conservative tempers exploded in a scene unprecedented in Parliament. When Churchill got up to speak, Mr. Balfour, the government leader, rose also from his place and walked out, followed by the massed ranks of the Conservative Party. A few weeks afterwards, Churchill took his seat with the Liberals.

Almost immediately there followed an election in which the Liberals came into power. Churchill was rewarded, to extreme Conservative fury, by government office. He was only the Under-Secretary of State for the Colonies, but then he was only thirty-one. Besides, his importance was increased by the fact that his superior sat in the House of Lords. It therefore fell to Churchill to pilot through the House of Commons the just and statesmanlike settlement which the Liberals now made with the Boers.

He did it so well that he was promoted. By 1911, he had been the president of the Board of Trade and was Home Secretary. He had written an excellent life of his father. He was newly married, a privy councilor, Ecclesiastical Commissioner, member of the Cabinet, and much in the public eye. His hair was receding and he looked very slightly plumper, but he was still in his thirties and happy as the day was long. A number of his colleagues were uncommonly brilliant men, and with the Liberals there was always something to be done.

He had married in 1908. Miss Clementine Hozier was of suitably similar background, granddaughter of a peer. She was pretty, strikingly well dressed, quiet in manner, but most intelligent. Her politics were Liberal, more so than Churchill's own; and on one occasion she walked out of Blenheim in a huff. In her own family, such awful things were not said! The wedding of a Cabinet Minister was quite an event, and the marriage proved perfectly happy. Winston Churchill was too uninhibited a man to be easy to live with. What he felt, he instantly expressed. Yet Clementine Churchill, amused but never ruffled, commanded his lifelong devotion.

Churchill's years with the Liberal ministry were dominated by his friendship with David Lloyd George. Both men had similarly quick minds, were emotional, had great gifts of verbal expression. Lloyd George, however, had been brought up in a small Welsh village by a shoemaker uncle. He was almost entirely self-taught and had started his political career as a Welsh nationalist. Broadening his interests with his experience, he was able in these years to trace the first faint outlines of what we now know as the Welfare State. Under his influence, Winston "discovered poverty" — as somebody treated to a burst of Churchillian eloquence sourly remarked. Indeed, it was almost literally true. He never had actually seen how poor people lived, and when he did so, his sense of compassion was powerfully stirred. Winston's compassion for the common man henceforward runs through his entire political life as a minor theme. It was never forgotten, though its personal quality was such that the organized working class did not do it justice. His achievements in these years were perfectly concrete: national labor exchanges, trade boards for regulating hours and conditions of work, boys' reformatories, various prison reforms, rules for safety in coal mines. The permanent officials of his department were completely taken aback by the number of new notions he could turn out in a day... most of them not much good to the experts, yet a surprising number sound. If one could bear the battery of his personality, he was a good man to work for, they noted. Things moved along when he was around.

Meanwhile, the public reaction to the lively personality of its youngest minister displayed a certain unease. In 1911, the London police, who do not wear arms, had the experience of pursuing a gang which shot it out. Several policemen were killed, and the criminals went to earth in a house on Sydney Street, where they barricaded themselves in for a long siege. This totally new situation was something of a crisis. The Home Secretary's office was informed, and Mr. Churchill, rushing down to interfere, gaily directed the clearing of houses nearby and the bringing up of soldiers complete with artillery. Next morning the public was treated to a photograph of the Home Secretary in top hat and fur-lined coat imperfectly sheltered in a doorway and peering across the street. As Mr. Balfour acidly remarked in Parliament, "I can understand what the photographer was doing in the danger zone, but why the Home Secretary?" The Minister's own comment to one of his permanent staff has a different ring. "Don't be croth, Charlie. It was such fun!"

Mr. Balfour was thought to have had the last word, and when the newsreels of the incident appeared, the minister was booed. For the ominous truth was that Churchill, in spite of his startling success, was not too popular. The Conservative Party blamed him far more than they did Lloyd George for the radical measures which the Liberal Party had forced through. After all, one could expect nothing better of a shoemaker's apprentice, while even Mr. Asquith was of mere middle-class background. Not so Churchill, who was thought to have betrayed his own kind for selfish ambition. Had not the Liberals bought him over by promising office?

Meanwhile, Churchill's position in the Liberal Party, though prominent, was not entirely secure. With a few great exceptions, he did not make intimate friends — owing to his habit of always wanting to talk about what interested him at the time. People found his enthusiasms a bore and some of his notions quite wild. Not understanding the mentality of a man who tested out his ideas in discussion, they rather suspected he was unreliable. Anyway, they were certain he was no radical at heart in spite of his record.

Such were the sentiments of Parliament vaguely diffused throughout the nation. Ill luck and a combination of these various sorts of ill-will had brought about a definite quarrel with the organized working class. At the end of 1910, there had been a Welsh coal strike in which feeling had run extremely high. There had been riots, and the authorities had asked for troops to maintain order. Churchill very wisely had responded by sending large numbers of extra police. He had, however, felt unable to refuse a request for armed men and had dispatched them with instructions that they be kept in reserve. Perhaps the authorities on the spot might have managed without them, perhaps not. At all events, on several occasions the soldiers were used and some few people were injured, though no one was killed. Workers all over the country were outraged. Pamphlets and speakers misrepresented the facts. Churchill, an aristocrat and ex-soldier, had called the military out to murder the workingman, and blood had been shed. It would cry for vengeance! Such stories haunted Churchill's political life for twenty years. The feeling engendered was further heightened about six months later on when a railway strike caused him to call out troops again. The idea was spreading that he overdramatized crises and made them worse. For the present, Churchill's position was so completely assured that these currents of opinion could not undermine it perceptibly. Yet it was a weakness in a democratic statesman that he should antagonize so many people and attach so few. Absorbed in a series of exciting ideas, it was always his tendency to be forgetful of people. Elevated by his surprising success, he was so now.

Into these pleasurable and active years now burst the crisis of Agadir. Plenty of people had agitated about German militarism before 1911, but Mr. Churchill had always preferred to ignore them. Even a government cannot spend money on everything at once, and this was a period when domestic politics had been absorbing. Besides, it was characteristic of Churchill that he gave his whole mind to what he was doing — rode his enthusiasms to death, as his enemies complained. Once he understood that there was a real danger of war, he had to go poking round for things to do. Thus he discovered that the Navy's supply of cordite was for some reason in his care as Home Secretary and was protected by a few rather casual watchmen. Somewhat hysterically, his colleagues thought, he telephoned the Navy and demanded protection at once from sabotage. Denied it, he called up the War Office and made himself a nuisance until a guard had to be sent. The Secret Service, who were also under his wing, were suddenly granted permission to open the letters of many suspected persons. By 1914, they had accumulated knowledge about the German spy system which came in useful.

Winston's colleagues by now must have become resigned to the fact that he always most enjoyed any part of his duties which threatened to impinge on somebody else's. Indeed, being an able set of men, they could afford to indulge him. If Winston was going to have this particular bee in his bonnet, they might as well use his energies. Nothing would ever divert his attention. He was already bombarding the Cabinet with memoranda about the coming war. Accordingly Churchill was offered a place on the Committee of Imperial Defence, which considered war problems. Here it transpired that British military experts had come to the conclusion from a study of the German railroad system and military depots that in the event of war, the German army would invade France through

Belgium. Since Britain, France, and Germany had signed a treaty guaranteeing Belgian neutrality, it seemed most probable that Britain would have to come in. Accordingly, staff talks between the British and French had taken place, involving no obligations, but working out what would be done in such a case. The British army, reorganized and brought up to date, was now ready with an expeditionary force which would be transported to France on the outbreak of such a war. But the Navy declared themselves unable, and indeed unwilling, to provide the transportation. This focused a spotlight on the Navy, in the light of which the government did not like what it beheld.

The last war of crucial importance which the British Navy had waged was with Napoleon. Since then, sailing ships had given way to steam, wooden planks to armor plate, cannon balls to high explosive. Technically the Navy was in a fine state of competence, while its officers were as efficient as any in the world. However, its strategy was out of date. There was no war staff and no general plan of educating officers for the highest command. Among the senior admirals there was dead wood. It was highly urgent that someone strong-minded should take the Navy in hand.

Mr. Asquith offered the position of First Lord of the Admiralty to Winston Churchill. He never made a better appointment or one that gave more pleasure. Hurling himself into his new duties, Winston talked technical matters until even Mr. Lloyd George showed signs of boredom. Mr. Asquith, inveigled aboard the Admiralty yacht — a happy possession — preferred to take his seat some distance off, where as a rival attraction he aired his extraordinary memory for facts by improving on the guidebook. Winston was elected an Elder Brother of Trinity House — that is, a member of the directing board of an ancient and respectable body which manages lighthouses, harbor pilots, and various other coast-guard activities. This carried the right to what its owner evidently thought a perfectly splendid uniform, including epaulettes, cocked hat, a gratifying number of naval buttons, and tails. He gaily dressed up to his part on solemn occasions.

Meanwhile, his industry was phenomenal. He had gone to the Admiralty to prepare for war with Germany. The general European situation was ominously simple. France and Russia, locked in alliance by fear of the German army, dared make no other enemies. It was only the Germans who challenged the might of Great Britain on the high seas. More specifically, Churchill was pledged to put through a change in naval strategy, create a war staff, replace some admirals in high command, and work in co-operation with the War Office. In other words, he knew quite generally what he needed to achieve, but the actual problems and the personnel of the Navy were utterly new. Nor could he wait to gather information for months or possibly years before he acted. Both processes must be carried on at once. He spent his weekends at Portsmouth or Devonport, looking over ships and asking officers of every rank from the fleet to lunch or dine. With the aid of the Admiralty yacht he managed to visit in the course of less than three years every dockyard, shipyard, and naval establishment belonging to Great Britain in the British Isles or the Mediterranean. He made himself personally familiar with every important ship. Meanwhile, in a general way he learned to master technical details concerning design, naval engines, naval artillery, armor plate, or even supply.

In taking action on naval matters, much depended on the choice of sound advisers. Chief among Churchill's was the extraordinary admiral, now retired and over seventy, whose lifelong struggle had brought about vast revolutions in naval gunnery and design and had forced through the adoption by the Navy of submarines. Admiral Fisher, one is inclined to hope, was a man unlike any other. Disagree with him on a matter concerning the Navy, and he declared war to the knife. He had literally ruined scores of careers and left behind him embittered feuds which were still doing their damage. He saw everything not simply in black and white, but in black and scarlet. To read Fisher's letters with their peculiar phrases, their exclamation points, underlinings and double underlinings is to wonder whether he were not really a madman. But there was no madness in his views on naval development or strategy. These were brilliant and sound. Fisher was a small man about Churchill's own height, with a body like a compact little barrel and an immense head with high, bald forehead and long, square, harsh, aggressive face. Perceiving that in Winston his own views had come to fresh life, Fisher now adopted him almost as a favorite son. His fiery letters with "yours till charcoal sprouts" or "till Hell freezes" make curious reading in the light of the famous quarrel which was to follow.

Churchill's first task was naturally the shake-up in high

personnel and the creation of a naval war staff. It is generally agreed that his arrangements were the best that could have been made. However, it is one thing to set up the framework for change and quite another to educate the commanders of a whole navy. Time only does that. Great Britain entered the war with excellent captains, but she suffered throughout from a lack of initiative in the higher commands. Meanwhile, however, naval strategy for the coming war was reviewed, and for the first two summers its problems were studied in grand maneuvers of the fleet.

Of equal importance with these were technical changes. Spurred by the German expansion, Britain was building twelve capital ships at this time, five of them within a year of completion, the others at various stages. These were to have been armed with thirteen-point-five-inch guns, which hurled a broadside of one and one half times the weight of the German twelves and had a very much larger excess of bursting power. To make things doubly sure, it was suggested that the guns be redesigned as fifteen-inch.

No fifteen-inch gun had been designed, much less built. Literally thousands of parts of the ships in construction would have to be scrapped and remade to fit. Testing would take a year; but if the Navy waited for this to be done, five ships must come off the ways with thirteen-point-fives. Should one be cautious and accept five ships with less than possible power? Or should one go ahead without testing out the fifteen-inch? The technical experts assured Churchill that as far as they knew the gun was sound; yet the price of failure would be tremendous and the responsibility his. He went ahead.

The use of the fifteen-inch brought up another question. Eight of these tremendous guns would nearly double the weight of the ten German twelves. Thus by sacrificing two guns with their vast mass of equipment, one might have more room for engines and greater speed. The conception of the fast battleship was thus born and brought with it the question of coal versus oil. Oil was recognized to be more efficient. It produced greater speeds, required no shoveling, and could be replenished by sea. Great Britain, however, had immense supplies of coal, but no oil. Moreover, the oil supplies of the world were in the hands of great trusts under foreign control. If the Navy were to change over to oil, it must be independent. For an answer Churchill turned to the Middle East. After negotiations, the British government invested money in development there, and the Anglo-Persian Oil Company was born. Storage tanks must now be constructed and vast reserves of oil laid in, while the new fast battleships and smaller oil-burning ships were all pushed on.

These technical changes are worth dwelling on because of the vigorous interest which Churchill took in them and because they demonstrate his daring, farsighted mind. They also involved him in the largest naval budgets of history to date, which had to be fought step by step through the Cabinet and through a Parliament which was Liberal, and therefore not imperially minded. Marshaling his forces with brilliant organization, Churchill was successful, while the very battle brought him incessantly before the public eye. His reputation was constantly and deservedly increasing. It seemed probable that if there were to be a war, he must go to the top. The war, however, lay as yet in the future, full of surprises.

Meanwhile, in response to further German efforts, a reorganization of the whole fleet was put in hand. This was intended to provide one fleet which was always ready; one partly in training and on call as it were, and a third which was to be manned by trained reserves. In pursuance of this arrangement, the 1914 summer maneuvers were canceled in favor of a huge test mobilization. When the international crisis came, Churchill had the moral courage to delay the scattering of the fleet for a few days. He hoped his action might give the Germans pause. It failed to do so, and in August, 1914, the war broke out. But in 1915, when Churchill fell from his high position more or less in disgrace, he received a farewell visit from Field Marshal Lord Kitchener, a man with whom he had worked and disagreed. Kitchener, it appears, had come for the simple purpose of doing justice to Churchill's achievements. "There is one thing they cannot take from you. The fleet was ready."

The Reversals of War | 4

THE GREAT alliances and the vast preparations for war bore their inevitable fruit in the First World War. The nations of Europe hurled themselves into conflict on a scale which had never been seen. In the midst of the struggle were massed the great powers of Central Europe, the modern German Empire, and the old-fashioned Austro-Hungarian. On the east these faced the Russians, and on the west France and Britain behind her. Lesser nations which were not yet involved held out and pondered the prospects of this side or of that, Italy leaning toward the Allied powers, and Turkey to the Germans. By most of the combatants little was yet understood of modern war, and much went wrong. The French, driven back to the very outskirts of Paris, lost forever their chance to fight it out on German soil. Meanwhile, the Germans had made their attack through Belgium at the cost of drawing in Great Britain because they expected by these means to win a quick war. They almost did so; and for a desperate six weeks, the eyes of the world were focused on their efforts.

Thus for the Allies in the west nothing went according to plan except Mr. Churchill's naval war. German commerce duly vanished from the high seas. The British Expeditionary Force was transported to France without loss of a man. Of over forty possible commerce raiders, all but five were speedily taken or chased into neutral ports and there interned. War-damage insurance went down to three per cent. Yet this success was expected, and meanwhile the naval victory which had been expected, too, did not come off. For Winston Churchill had done his work too well. The German Imperial Fleet, outgunned and outnumbered, remained in its harbors awaiting the issue of the land war, while the main force of the British patrolled the mists of the North Sea like a cat at a mousehole.

The situation of British naval power thus greatly lacked drama as compared to the struggle in France, while unluckily for Churchill such drama as appeared brought credit to the Germans. Almost a dozen German warships had been in foreign stations when war broke out, and the task of hunting them down proved far from easy. The British navy, with its main strength tied up in the North Sea, had also to convoy the regular troops from India and elsewhere to France, and take territorials out to replace them. Australia, Canada, and New Zealand needed escorts for the troops they were sending to Europe. Expeditions against Samoa, German New Guinea, and nearly a dozen outposts of the German Empire were under way. These tasks were complicated by the necessity of having in every case a ship superior to the cruiser it might meet, not only in gun power, but wherever possible in speed. Meanwhile, the actual hunting of *Emden* in the Indian Ocean, of *Goeben* in the Mediterranean, and of *Scharnhorst* and *Gneisenau* in the vast reaches of the Pacific went on with indifferent success. *Emden* had a merry life in the Bay of Bengal and did so much damage that twenty ships had to be brought into the search for her. Through an excess of caution by the admirals in command, *Goeben* got away to Constantinople, where her arrival decided Turkey to enter the war as a German ally. In the Pacific, on the other hand, Admiral Cradock discarded the battleship which had been given him for protection because it was too slow. Thus falling on *Scharnhorst* and *Gneisenau* with inadequate forces, he was utterly destroyed. After this, some two dozen warships of greatly superior metal had to be employed to hunt these two vessels and their three attendant light cruisers. Unquestionably the weakness of the Navy lay in its commanders.

The *Emden's* successes against British merchantmen angered the public out of all proportion to their value, while the disaster of Admiral Cradock at Coronel was a great shock. Churchill's position was far from enviable, since for security reasons he could not defend his arrangements. Moreover, he had gained little credit for the swiftness with which the Navy had cleared the seas of German merchant ships. The general public had taken his success here as a matter of course. If, however, Churchill had been willing to let temporary setbacks be forgotten in the general success of naval strategy, all might have been well. He could not do so. The future of England manifestly hung on the struggle in France and might be decided in a month or a few more weeks. All Churchill's generous instincts bade him lend a hand, and his resourcefulness suggested methods. In fact, disposing of forces of one sort and another which could be used on land, Churchill was only too eager for his own good to involve them without much regard for military conventions. Thus minor adventures on the coast of France to some extent diverted his attention from naval affairs and gave him a reputation for rashness. Naturally his help was not asked save in desperation, so that the operations in which he became involved could bring him small credit.

The British air force before the war had consisted of a flying corps and a naval air service. The former and larger was intended to provide for the defense of Great Britain. To this it was quite inadequate now, since every machine was needed in France. The naval air service, thanks to Churchill's personal interest, was in good shape. He was delighted to use it for the defense of the country against the German airship, the Zeppelin. These Zeppelins with their great bladder of highly inflammable gas were vulnerable objects wherever they could be reached, but they flew higher than an airplane could climb to intercept them. On the other hand Zeppelin hangars were conspicuous for their size. If British air bases could be moved to the coast of France where the range would be shorter, it might be possible to destroy these monsters on the ground. Accordingly, Churchill set up a naval air base at Dunkirk with the intention of connecting with advanced fields farther inland.

At this point in the line, the flanks of both armies had formed a fluid front. Small cavalry parties of Germans were actually penetrating within a few miles of Dunkirk, terrorizing the country without really holding it down. The Royal Navy, being unable for all its resource to lay its hand on cavalry, resorted under Churchill's inspiration to armored cars. This new experiment in war was highly successful up to the point where the Germans began to dig trenches across the roads. Undaunted, Churchill called on his designers for an armored car which would cross a trench. Various types were produced, among which one with caterpillar treads appeared most promising. By this time, however, the armies had dug themselves in from the sea to the Switzerland border. Dismayed by the growing complexity of trench fortifications, the generals were not interested in what was to become the tank. However, Churchill pushed experiment on for another few months while he had the power. He thus became the real father, though not the inventor of one weapon which in the course of World War I revolutionized tactics.

Meanwhile, the threat of the Germans penetrating in force to Dunkirk and Calais grew. Resourceful once more, Churchill took a brigade of marines and threw them in, making them mobile by buses from the London streets and using them for demonstrations in as many places as possible to give the impression that the coast was strongly held. This "Dunkirk Circus," as it now came to be called, was felt by conventional people to be taking the time of the First Lord from his proper business. Being Churchill, he could not leave such a risky affair to its commander, but had to take time out to visit and make his suggestions. Mr. Asquith, who in the last resort must be appealed to over naval business when Churchill was away, became annoyed. His high opinion of Churchill's abilities was slightly clouded for the first time by doubt of his judgment. Others more or less in the know shook their heads and brought up the sinking of three British cruisers by one submarine on the Dogger Bank patrol. It happened that Churchill had mentioned the danger in this routine; and the Admiralty War Staff was to blame for the tragedy, not he. But charges stick.

The first phase of the land war in France was finally decided by the Battle of the Marne in early September. Germany was not to have her quick victory after all and might as well turn her efforts to securing what definite prizes she could while the fronts were still fluid. Accordingly the conflict rolled northwestward, both sides racing for the sea and the Channel ports, Calais, Dunkirk, Ostend, and north of all of them, strategically worth all the rest, the port of Antwerp. This was a fortified town and was defended by the remains of the Belgian army, which was however no match for the German. On October the second, the Belgian government notified the Cabinet that they were about to evacuate the town, lest they be entirely cut off. Mr. Asquith chanced to be away. An agitated meeting took place between Churchill, Lord Kitchener, the Secretary for War, and Lord Grey, the Foreign Secretary. They felt that somehow or other, and in spite of the fierceness of the struggle now going on elsewhere, help must be found for Antwerp. If the town would only hold out for a few days, this could be forthcoming. Yet presumably the Belgians knew their situation best and could not be dictated to by telegrams. Someone must go over.

Churchill's self-confidence, undamaged so far by events, led him to volunteer. Lord Kitchener agreed. The case was desperate, and Winston put everything into it that he

had, including drama. An American correspondent described his manner at Belgian headquarters as being for all
the world like that of the hero who arrives in the nick of
time in an old-fashioned thriller. Perceiving, moreover,
that he would have to put heart into military men, he had
donned uniform himself — the undress uniform of an Elder
Brother of Trinity House. With his usual magnificent unselfconsciousness, he paid no attention to the fact that people in England who knew what this uniform was might
find it comic. A story has circulated since that when
queried about this peculiar costume, Churchill made answer in his limited, schoolboy French, "Je suis le frère aîné de
la Trinité." This calls up a picture of a Frenchman clasping
his head in despair and exclaiming, "Mon Dieu!"

In spite of the presence of the Belgian king, the government, and the remains of the army, Winston in a few hours
was the soul of Antwerp's defense. It was a startling tribute
to his personality, but could not have been accomplished
by pure bounce. Telegrams were furiously passing between
him and Lord Kitchener, who was able to promise a mixed
force of fifty-three thousand to be thrown against the Germans from the south as soon as it was ready. Meanwhile,
if the lines before Antwerp could just hold out...The
Belgian army later proved to have fight left in it; but at
the moment it was worn out, demoralized, and crumbling.
Immediate assistance inside Antwerp itself must be given,
and by fresh troops. Churchill suggested the Royal Naval
Division, which he himself had recently formed because the
Navy had more volunteers than it could use on shipboard at
this moment. True, the division was not more than half

trained and could not maneuver, but men were wanted now to fight in entrenchments. The crucial point was the Naval Division could be sent over in a matter of hours, since it was not a question of having to withdraw them from the line.

The Royal Naval Division was sent. Churchill, perceiving that Antwerp would collapse without him, now wired over that he would resign from the Admiralty if he could be appointed to command the Antwerp defense. He explained that he had not imagined he would need to remain more than twenty-four hours, but he now realized that he could not perform both duties. Mr. Asquith, who had not been consulted on Churchill's going to Antwerp, was a sober man who did not find it funny that Churchill, a cavalry lieutenant, should be asking command over major generals. His Cabinet colleagues, who thought nothing humorous in the present crisis, were merely outraged that Winston should be neglecting his vital job for other people's. Only Lord Kitchener, the sole military man in the Cabinet itself, was not scornful of the suggestion.

Winston was ordered to return; but before he could do so, the exhausted Belgians broke, and Antwerp fell. His valiant efforts had prolonged the siege for exactly five days. The Belgian army with its King and government got away, but part of the Royal Naval Division was forced to take refuge in the neutral territory of Holland, where it was interned.

The defense of Antwerp for these five days and the rush to its rescue are now quite generally agreed to have saved the Channel ports. In other words, Churchill's effort was of crucial importance and well worth making. All this, however, could not be understood in the general confusion. What the public saw at the time was that he had gone charging off, proclaiming that Antwerp would be held... and had lasted five days. He had thrown in half-trained troops and was responsible for a third of them being interned for the rest of the war. None of this was his job, which he had in fact neglected, to indulge himself in drama. A general feeling was gaining ground that Churchill's character was dangerously wild.

Criticism of the Navy was growing, too; and it expressed itself in a curious way. The Director of Naval Operations, known in Great Britain as the First Sea Lord, was Louis of Battenberg, a German princeling who had served over forty years in the British Navy. There could be no question of Prince Louis' loyalty, but the public now chose to pretend that there was. He was forced to resign, and his going revealed to Churchill something of his own precarious position. He needed a powerful supporter to replace Prince Louis and found him in Admiral Fisher, then seventy-four, but as fiery as ever. Fisher and Churchill together made a strange team. The old man, who did not sleep well, got up at 4 A.M. and worked till late afternoon. Churchill preferred to work at night and now adapted his hours to suit Fisher's. He got up before noon and went to bed at two or three in the morning. Thus between them they manned the Admiralty more or less round the clock. Moreover, in spite of the fact that they both were domineering, they worked in complete harmony — no doubt very largely because they still happened to hold the same point of view.

The year 1914 ran out after witnessing casualties on the British and French side alone of almost a million. Yet the forces of the nations were not nearly exhausted, though a curious deadlock had paralyzed their war. The German navy still lurked in its harbors. On land, the armies were dug into trenches facing each other for the whole length of their border. Flanking movements no longer came into question. Barbed-wire entanglements prevented surprise. What was to be done? The civilian directors and the military chiefs of the war now began to diverge in a fashion which almost wrecked their common cause in the end. For the generals, the answer lay in vast supplies of high-explosive shell. Scatter the entanglements! Blow up the enemy's trenches! After shattering bombardment, send infantry across! To be sure our casualties will be high, perhaps higher than the German; but then we have more men. Besides, what alternative have we? We need to destroy the enemy's army in order to win the war — and his army is here.

Thus spoke the military mind, ignorant as yet of the Tank and oppressed by the practical problems of maintaining their own line or of pleasing the French. For as long as the Germans lay entrenched in the soil of France, it naturally followed that to Frenchmen the object of war was getting this back. The British Cabinet could afford to take a more detached view, but it was conscious of being in the power of its army chiefs to some extent. Were

they not the specialists? Oppressed by his amateur standing, Asquith held back. It was natural therefore that
Churchill's bolder temperament and his position at the
Admiralty should qualify him to take a strong lead in
introducing a plan.

There are always flanks in war. If the German position
in France could not be turned on land, what was naval
power for? By standing resolutely on the defensive in
France and using her navy to mount an attack elsewhere,
Great Britain might break up the German power more surely
than by draining oceans of blood in the trenches of Flanders.
Such general views were common to Lloyd George, to
Churchill, to Asquith, and indeed to numerous others. No
coherent policy had emerged, partly because Asquith had
not shown himself able to simplify government at the top
level in order to deal with the war. Thus everyone had
put forward his own pet scheme, while Asquith played
umpire and nothing was determined.

On the second of January, 1915, a decisive event took
place. The Grand Duke Nicholas of Russia, commander-
in-chief of her armies, made a formal request to Great
Britain for aid. The war in the East was not going well.
The Russian forces had proved themselves superior to the
Austro-Hungarian army, but unequal even to the forces
which the Germans then could spare. Moreover, Russian
industrial strength was inadequate to the problem of equip-
ping her armies for a long war on a modern scale. Unless
the Allies could mount some diversion this spring, disaster
might follow.

The collapse of Russia at this stage would probably mean

the loss of the war, and it was obvious that something ought to be done. It was against this background of Russian need and French stalemate that Churchill introduced a momentous plan.

Eighty per cent of Russia's sea-borne trade before the war had come through the Black Sea and into the Mediterranean, passing first through the straits of the Bosporus at Constantinople, then down the little Sea of Marmora and through the Dardanelles, the narrow waters which divide the Asiatic from the European shore. This passage to Russia had now been closed by the adherence of Turkey to the German side, leaving only the far northern ports of Archangel and Murmansk as an Allied supply line. It is not too much to say that if the Allies had been able to pour supplies at will through the Dardanelles to Russia, the whole course of the war and of the Russian Revolution must have been different.

In January, 1915, the final Russian collapse lay far in the future; yet even discounting her call for help, the whole position of the Dardanelles in the eastern war was crucial. The Turkish Empire, stretching from Eastern Europe through Asia Minor and the Middle East to the borders of Egypt, had long been moribund. It was passionately hated by the various states of the Balkans which had once been under its rule. These little countries were wondering which side to join. They were, moreover, in some respects the key to Austria-Hungary as well as to Turkey. Such, however, were their rivalries among themselves that only a conviction of the overpowering might of Great Britain would serve to unite them. Meanwhile, the Turkish government was corrupt and insecure. A push in the right place might send it over.

For all these various reasons, Churchill's conception of using British naval power to open the Dardanelles was the most imaginative strategical idea of the war. The narrow strait was protected by several elderly forts, and it was probable that the Turks had moved up some field artillery also. On the European side, a mountainous peninsula called Gallipoli, never more than a few miles across, protrudes from Europe parallel to the Asiatic shore. This was almost roadless and certainly not long before was undefended. A British army might take it by surprise if promptly assembled and without giving Turkey due warning.

Lord Kitchener, backing up the generals, refused to spare a man from France; and from his authority at this time there was no appeal. But the Mediterranean fleet contained old battleships, due to go on the scrapheap and yet fitted of course with powerful guns. Sound naval practice forbade a ship to take on forts; but the forts of the Dardanelles were obsolete. And one of the surprises of the war to date had been the German howitzers knocking out the Belgian defense forts one by one. Considering, therefore, that the ships were expendable, might they not be used to force the straits by naval bombardment? Once the fleet got into the Sea of Marmora, Constantinople, sprawling, unfortified, and mixed in population, was easy prey. The only factories of ammunition in Turkey were right on the shore. Churchill put this scheme to the admiral commanding in the area, who with some reservations thought it might work. To the Cabinet, Churchill explained that naval action, unlike a formal expedition, could be broken off midway without loss of prestige. The Cabinet, still trembling between all sorts of alternatives, was only too happy to have the best of both worlds in this fashion. A naval attack on the Dardanelles was therefore agreed.

From this small beginning grew the Gallipoli expedition in which a quarter of a million British, Australians, and New Zealanders died in 1915, together with an equal number of Turks. From its final failure sprang the defeat of Russia, the Communist Revolution, the endless, futile bloodshed in France, the ruin of the Balkan States, the wearisome and costly campaigns in Syria and Greece. For as its success had promised great rewards, so its failure brought grief and disaster to the Allies on the largest scale. It pulled down Asquith and Kitchener, gave the strategy more firmly into the hands of the generals, degraded Churchill first from the Admiralty, and then altogether from office. It blasted his reputation to greater or lesser extent for twenty-five years. The Dardanelles had been Churchill's plan — both the naval engagement which did not force the straits, and the expedition when Kitchener changed his mind and spared the men too late. What use is imagination unless the judgment which goes with it is sound? For rash or hasty men in war there is no place.

Yet the Dardanelles was so nearly won that reading over the records of both sides, it is possible to pick out several moments when a single piece of bad luck or bad judgment turned the scale. In fact, one is almost tempted to say mere luck prevailed. As for the many errors of detail which the

British made, they were none of them Churchill's. In fact, the general plan was sound enough. Churchill's error lay in demanding too much from the British governmental machine.

The adaptation of Great Britain to war presented problems which the other combatant nations did not have to face. Her tiny volunteer army had meant that everything, including man-power and supply, was on a small scale. The vast expansion which was called for all of a sudden set up strain and stress which was felt on every level of national life. Nowhere was this dislocation more evident than in Asquith's Cabinet, which found itself no longer in complete control of affairs. Having raised its generals to the status of national heroes, chiefly for the purpose of a huge recruiting drive, it dared not dismiss them. Moreover, its own powerful personalities, whatever their department, now regarded the war as their common concern and all had views. Thus Asquith was undermined both from within and from without. Churchill himself was at a still greater remove from real power. He could and did convince Asquith, but the Prime Minister felt unable to dictate immediate action. Meanwhile, other politicians regarded the Dardanelles scheme as being only Churchill's and not necessarily better than their own. Everyone had to be persuaded, and everything was done piecemeal, haphazard. Forces were committed on a great scale, but never quite enough at once or quite in time. Churchill's mistake, and it was a very great one, lay in not perceiving that he was dragging men on against their will. It was born of his self-confidence and his enthusiastic nature. It grew and was fostered by the confusion of those times. Many people already had remarked that Churchill was overeager in pushing an idea, that his torrents of eloquence were apt to roll over the opposition without converting it. Now for the first time his wonderful fire betrayed him.

Nor was this all. Inside the Admiralty, Churchill was fighting very much the same sort of battle that Asquith was doing with the military men. He was the civilian head of the Admiralty, and it developed that in some respects the naval staff had different views. The German navy, still inaccessible and undefeated, was the only instrument which could win a war with Great Britain in one afternoon. It must at all times be matched by a British North Sea fleet so much more powerful that no mistakes and no bad luck could affect the issue. So far Churchill and his naval staff were agreed. There is no doubt, however, that Churchill felt the admirals were too cautious. Facts and figures seemed to make no difference to their instinct for piling up strength. It was becoming clear that England's admirals took their responsibilities hard. In March, Admiral de Roebeck was to break off his attempt to force the Dardanelles on the very edge of success because three of his out-of-date ships were sunk by mines. Navy authorities at home expressed the fear that a large operation in the Mediterranean would sooner or later demand reinforcements from the main fleet.

As usual, the Dardanelles scheme was not the only one before the Navy. Fisher had his eye set on a perilous operation off the German coast by which he hoped to force the German navy to make a sally in strength. He therefore

took a negative stand about the Dardanelles. He and his
naval staff did agree to support an army landing on Gallipoli, but they considered the suggestion of forcing the
Dardanelles strait by the old battleships would not be
practicable. Fisher was talked over by Winston's enthu-
siasm and Kitchener's authority, but never convinced. He
felt, as others were to feel, that Winston's personality had
crowded him into consent against his will. In this way,
Fisher found himself in a position to take credit if things
went well and to say "I told you so" if they went ill. When
in fact they did go ill and the scale of the operation was
increased again and again, Fisher began to grow angry.
What is more, he began to grow jealous. Here he was,
recognized to be England's greatest sailor, full of experience and years, not even head of the Admiralty, not even
a member of the War Cabinet. Meanwhile, Lord Kitchener,
whose reputation as a soldier was no more assured, ran
the War Office just as he pleased with no one to contradict
him, not even Asquith. Who was Churchill but an amateur
of a few years' experience, Fisher's own pupil, who now
thought he knew it all? Churchill was devoting resources
to the Dardanelles fleet which should be concentrating on
the submarine menace now just beginning to be felt in
home waters. He took too much on himself. When Fisher
got to his desk at four in the morning, he might find a
paper minuted during the night in Churchill's red ink,
"For immediate action. First Lord to see later." It would
undoubtedly concern itself with something which they two
had already discussed in general terms; but in discussion
Fisher got the worst of things, or felt he did so. He was

determined that the Navy should be recalled from the whole Dardanelles operation.

On the fifteenth of May, Hell finally froze and charcoal sprouted. The two domineering characters clashed head on. Fisher blew up. He shot in his resignation and simply disappeared. Tracked down and persuaded that it was at least his duty to be available until his successor was appointed, he retired to his official residence and pulled down the shades. Not even the tidings that the German fleet was coming out of harbor changed his mind.

At Fisher's resignation, the political storm which had long been gathering broke. The Conservative Party, prodded by certain generals, had been mounting a campaign against Churchill's military adventures. Conservative papers were publishing daily attacks on his judgment, his flair for the dramatic, his bouncing, self-confident personality, and his unorthodox methods. But these were his enemies. Now in the hour of trial, Churchill discovered that he really had few friends. Absorbed in the conduct of the war, he had neglected Parliament, and even the Liberal members held this against him.

Asquith did not fall from power at once, but he might better have done so. A coalition government was formed in which all parties were to have a voice. As a price for consenting to act under Asquith, the Conservatives demanded that Winston be dismissed from the Admiralty. Few people objected. Only Kitchener and one other of his colleagues came to see him while he waited for his successor in a deserted office, fiddling with papers which were no longer his concern, and finished at forty.

He was offered the position of Chancellor of the Duchy of Lancaster, which is an office carrying no ministerial duties. It is usually given to a junior politician and in Churchill's case was an insult. He accepted it, however, as it still gave him a chance to be heard in council. The army invasion of Gallipoli had by now taken place, after the Turks had been warned and allowed time to dig themselves in. At the cost of much bloodshed, three small beachheads had been established and were still maintained. It still was possible that if these were reinforced, the place might be taken.

The cause of Gallipoli was the only object that Churchill now struggled for, but it was doomed. The size of the war council had to be increased so that party representation could find a place on it. This made it unwieldy, and besides most matters were treated as party affairs. Decisions were worse than before and harder to arrive at. Help was sent to Gallipoli too late again. Other projects began to seem more attractive. The management of the war went from bad to worse, and Asquith had manifestly lost control. Unpopular, distrusted, powerless, Churchill strove against this current; but for the first time in his political life his footing was lost. When it was decided to give up, accept defeat, and evacuate the Gallipoli army, his work was over and he resigned. He was not yet forty-one, and his life lay in ruins. The general verdict appeared to be that his great talents, his industry, his desire to serve his country were spoiled by one tremendous flaw of character. He was dangerous as the plague. The flower of England's youth had died on account of his errors. It seemed impossible that Winston Churchill should rise to influence in his country's affairs again. A career which was to have been made by the war was utterly ended.

A LITTLE, round-faced, stoop-shouldered man was beginning again in his forties and finding it hard. Half a dozen
newspapers would have outbid each other to hire his brilliant pen. His organizing talents must have been well paid
in industry, had he cared for money. But civilian jobs in a
war were not for Winston Churchill. If he could no longer
direct, then he would fight.

He had visions of military glory. Having risen so early
to the top, having always known top people, he thought
quite naturally in terms of high command. He was expecting to begin with a brigade. Meanwhile, however, he was
to spend a month in the trenches with the Grenadier Guards
as a sort of senior apprentice to study conditions. He joined
them on a grim November day of 1915 to find a reception in keeping with the life and with the weather. The
Colonel did not say much, but what he did say was
devastating. "I think I ought to tell you that we were not
consulted at all on the matter of your coming to join us."

Undismayed, Churchill spent his month winning over the
Grenadiers; but he did not get the brigade which had been
half promised. Questions were asked about him in Parliament, and Mr. Asquith warned the commander-in-chief that
Churchill's appointment to anything more than a battalion
would cause comment. There was nothing for it but to

swallow chagrin and attend to a job which he felt was a waste of his time. For all the influence a lieutenant colonel had on the course of the war, one might just as well have become an infantry private.

A battalion of the Sixth Royal Scots Fusiliers was by no means happy to find that their new colonel was the notorious politician whose arrival in the trenches a month ago had made such a stir. Churchill did not, however, waste time in finding out how they felt. He gathered his officers together and declared immediate war on the lice which were generally considered a necessary evil of trench life. The men were amused, then impressed, and then furiously busy in ways which never seemed to end. Long before one notion — good or bad — had been tried out, Churchill came up with another. They thought him sometimes unreasonable, but they had to like him, and they noticed that he worked even harder than they. His peculiar figure in an experimental waterproof suit, a French tin helmet, and a patent revolver which nearly shot his foot off one day could be met inspecting the trenches at any time till the early hours of the morning. He had a charmed life and was quite devoid of fear. Indeed, he liked danger.

Seeing no reason to be uncomfortable for its own sake, Churchill had stocked the mess with good cigars and brandy, which must have been useful, since he drew visitors like a magnet. Politicians or generals appeared to talk half the night about issues which really no longer concerned a lieutenant colonel. The thought was depressing, and the job he was doing seemed even less worth while. True, he had written a paper on the proper use of tanks and had sent it to the Committee of Imperial Defence; but there was no reason why his advice should be followed now. The unfamiliarity of the life and the challenge of war had produced an exhilaration which soon began to wear off. The general conduct of the war was going from bad to worse, and friends were beginning to tell him he ought to be in Parliament, pressing reforms.

In March he could bear it no longer and came home briefly to speak on the naval estimates. In June, his battalion was amalgamated with another so that he was out of a job. He applied for release from the army, and the Secretary of War, weighing anxiously the awkwardness of refusing or of consenting, agreed. In June he came home.

The last six months of 1916 mark perhaps the lowest point in a career which is full of ups and downs. Churchill's return to Parliament was ill received. People said he had very soon had too much of the trenches, and they spoke of his hunger for office as vulgar ambition. Jealously watched and bitterly hated, he had to stand idly by while the war went wrong. In the five months' Battle of the Somme, the British army was attempting to shatter the enemy's line regardless of cost. Its bloody failure merely drew upon Churchill the anger of those who directed affairs. His criticisms were brushed aside. His favorite brain-child, the tank, was completely misused. Feeling that he could have and would have done better, Churchill was condemned to look on while other men bungled.

In the previous year when he left the Admiralty, he had found himself with a most unwelcome amount of time on his hands. He was not a man of hobbies. As a cavalry subaltern in India, he had learned to play polo really well; and in spite of a shoulder which was apt to go out of joint, he still liked a game. He entertained a great deal, but generally with the notion of meeting some expert or trying out some theory. Recreation merely meant turning from administrative work to some other kind, to an article perhaps, an inspection of the fleet, or the Dunkirk Circus. In fact, as war went on, recreation and work had become indistinguishable. Quite suddenly both were cut off. The Duchy of Lancaster had no special duties. Winston Churchill, an impatient man at the best of times, could be counted on for a rage with nothing to do.

One horrible Sunday, he had picked up the children's paints and fiddled a little. On Monday, he charged out to buy some canvases, oils, brushes, and easel ... all the trimmings. He took them out to set them up and thought to himself, "Well, the sky is safe enough. One paints it blue." Cautiously he dipped a brush in blue and made a small mark.

"Painting?" It was Lady Lavery, wife of a well-known artist. She came over to look and asked him what he was hesitating about. She demanded a nice, big brush, filled it with paint, and slapped it on in sweeping strokes. It dawned on Winston that he could pile onto the canvas all the bold, bright colors he liked in generous masses. An amateur artist was suddenly born.

Painting was a splendid recreation, needing of course a special costume, a beach umbrella, maybe two, a shade on the easel, brushes, palettes, boxes growing heavier and larger with all the paraphernalia of gadgets. It was really satisfying, absorbing, different, and took time. Churchill made a bold artist with a fine sense of glowing color, but a certain heaviness, revealing perhaps a lack of technique in design, or a lack of talent. He became good enough to get into exhibitions under various false names, and anyway it did not matter. A healthy mind had found a healthy outlet.

Churchill did a good deal of painting in 1916 while things went from bad to worse and the government tottered. He needed solace in his private life, and he was fortunate in having exactly the wife that suited him, lively children, and the means to live as he pleased. Not that he considered himself well off, though his earnings at various times had been large. He believed in comfort, a good wardrobe, expensive cigars. He needed service. Secretaries were shamelessly worked to death and liked it. Entertaining was a part of daily life for Mrs. Churchill. Thus the routine went on, though the reason for it had gone, perhaps never to return. He was more unhappy than his friends had ever seen him, yet he could not now abandon his profession. He had tried to do so, but affairs of state drew him back, even though without power.

In December Asquith fell and was replaced by Lloyd George, Churchill's old friend and colleague. But the Conservatives, with whose help Asquith had been overthrown, would not hear of office for Churchill. It was not until July, 1917, that Lloyd George ventured to make him Minister of Munitions. Such was the outcry that it almost seemed as though the government would fall. In vain was it pointed out that as a minister of supply, Churchill could have no say in strategy. He was dangerous and, so the Conservatives said, out for personal ends. The radical wing of the working class had never loved him either.

Lloyd George held power till 1922, five crowded years including the last desperate struggles of war, the sudden victory, the long negotiations with the Allied powers at Versailles, the treaty of peace, and the various crises which the process of adjustment forced on Europe. It was a strange climax for the anti-imperialist, the radical who had pressed readjustment of wealth in the interests of the poor. It made him and destroyed him, lost him the confidence of his old friends without gaining him new ones. Never again in eighteen years did Lloyd George hold any office. Meanwhile, however, he reigned supreme, gathering power to make decisions from the very fact that lack of it had ruined Asquith. Thus what the Conservatives feared did come to pass. Inside the Cabinet there grew up an inner ring, consisting only of Lloyd George, Churchill, and the Earl of Birkenhead. The influence of Churchill, though never supreme, did shape some policy. His actual positions as Minister of Munitions, Minister of War, or Secretary of State for the Colonies tended to vary with what needed urgently to be done. His achievements and his failures were on an important scale.

The Ministry of Munitions was a very large organization when Churchill took it over. It had been created by Lloyd George for the purpose of converting industry to war, and its success was mainly the reason why Lloyd George stepped in the end into Asquith's shoes. Some reorganization Churchill did, but the chief interest of the position was that three months earlier, unarmed and unprepared, America had entered the war. Churchill's direct acquaintance with America dated from his famous lecture tour of 1901. He had, however, always been interested in the country of his mother, while his resourceful, extrovert personality made a natural appeal to American people. The friendship which he now established by correspondence with his opposite number, Bernard Baruch, became a lifelong connection. Vast agreements between the two countries were worked out. At the end of the struggle, Churchill was awarded the Distinguished Service Medal, and was the only Englishman to receive it.

For the rest, he pushed ahead his own particular interests, the tanks and the air force. In fact, he began to fly himself — a most dangerous proceeding, as he made no sort of allowance for the point of view of machines. They merely existed to do what he wanted, no matter how sudden the impulse which happened to move him. The Ministry had establishments in France; and Churchill discovered that he could gallop through his work in the morning, fly over at lunchtime, spend the afternoon at the front, and be back for an evening of work. He found this strenuous program exciting, possibly the more so because planes — even flown by somebody else — were very uncertain. He had several narrow escapes from death, once over the Channel when they just got back to France, and three or four forced landings with more or less of a crash. On one occasion he crashed from a hundred feet, stepped out of the wreckage, and two hours later was speaking in the House of Commons as though nothing had happened.

The Ministry came to an end with the war, and Lloyd George transferred him to the War Ministry to take care of demobilization. Unfair arrangements had caused near-mutiny among the troops, and Churchill's powers of organization were needed to set things right. This task he speedily performed, but far more important were his efforts during this time to turn the clock back in Russia.

The collapse of the Russian Empire had been followed by a liberal revolution which in turn was overthrown by extremists. Russia dissolved into anarchy with various parties fighting to impose their own point of view and liquidate the rest. This situation was complicated by the fact that Russia and Germany were still at war. Accordingly, in 1917, the Bolshevik extremists signed a treaty giving Germany whatever she cared to ask for in return for peace. This arrangement enabled the Germans to concentrate their forces on the Western Front, and the Bolsheviks to employ theirs in the internal struggle.

Very naturally this almost friendly arrangement between the Bolsheviks and the Germans was denounced by Russia's allies who were still fighting on. Very naturally also, the anti-Bolshevik Russians were outraged by the shameful terms of the treaty. Thus the two injured parties, the Western Allies and the various moderate or conservative groups in Russia, made common cause for the general purpose of keeping Russia in the war. By 1918, the Allies had also landed forces to protect their own considerable supply dumps which had been piled up for the benefit of the Tsarist war effort. Thus by the time war came to an end, they were very largely committed to armed interference.

Anti-Bolshevik forces which had been encouraged or even supplied by the Allies faced extinction if support which once had been offered was now withdrawn.

No one seemed quite to know what to do except Winston Churchill. His point of view was simple. The Bolshevik tyranny, imposed by mass terror, did not represent the Russian people. Furthermore, its communist doctrines were a danger, in the chaos which then existed, to all Eastern Europe. If the Allies would use their military strength in co-operation with the liberal elements in Russia, a sound regime could be set up. This in itself would be a powerful contribution to the peace of the twentieth century.

It seems not unlikely, looking back on the situation, that Churchill was right. He was also, however, demanding the impossible. The Allied armies were determined to go home. The expenses of war, borne for so long, were unendurable for another moment. British commanders did not speak Russian, and even those on the spot had really no notion of how to make sense out of what seemed to them to be chaos. The strength of the Bolshevik party lay in its unity. Against it were massed all shades of opinion from pink to purest white; that is, from socialist to Tsarist. One splinter party intrigued against another. One staked its claim out here, one there. In any case, foreign aid was naturally suspect. The Bolsheviks, who had started by betraying Russian interests, speedily became the party of patriots resenting interference.

The end was a natural one. The Allied governments did just enough to arouse resentment and expose their partisans to massacre. Then pulling out, they left the field clear for the Communist Party. Churchill for his part had showed no signs of learning the method by which England was to be governed between the two wars. He had not waited for the electorate to catch up with him before pressing on it a policy which he thought was right. At this moment when the whole country longed for peace, when the ethics of interfering in Russia looked dubious, when his own unpopularity was by no means a thing of the past, the Minister of War swam strongly against the stream.

At the Colonial Office, Churchill's work was more successful. The Middle East was in an uproar. That part of the Turkish Empire had been the scene of much fighting in which the Arabs, led by the Emir Feisal and the Englishman Lawrence, had asserted Arab independence. During the negotiations for peace, it appeared that the great powers had made contradictory promises to different peoples and that larger interests were going to be satisfied first. Lawrence furiously proclaimed that the Arabs were betrayed. The Emir Feisal seized Damascus, from which the French threw him out by force. The Middle East seethed with vendettas, sectional interests, nationalism, and feelings of all sorts at white-hot heat. There seemed no reason why the situation should ever make sense or ever be tranquil.

Churchill's answer was to get hold of Lawrence and persuade him to offer his knowledge of the Arab world and his advice. Lawrence, a very strange man, was disillusioned with postwar governments and hard to draw out of his shell. Churchill was persuasive, however, and a committee of experts was summoned to consult with himself and Lawrence in Cairo. The journey was exciting. At one time Churchill's train was mobbed and its windows smashed by stones; at another he was almost mowed down by hordes of enthusiasts. Private life became impossible, since a bodyguard was never more than a few feet away — though as a concession he stood outside the door while the Minister wallowed in his bath. Spirits rising to meet these emergencies, Churchill snatched odd moments for the things he felt a man ought not to miss, such as painting the Pyramids, visiting Gethsemane, or learning how to ride a camel and coming a cropper. The settlement which he worked out satisfied the Arabs by making the Emir Feisal king of Iraq and his brother king of Transjordan. Meanwhile, the British army in the Middle East was replaced by an air corps which cost far less to keep up and proved more effective. The Arab world settled down to peace for many years.

No less fundamental and far more vivid to England was the old, perennial problem of Irish rights. It would be impossible to explain how bitter an issue the Irish question had become in English political life. In 1914, the Liberal Party had passed an Irish Home Rule Act which had literally brought both countries to the verge of civil war. So far beyond reason had feeling gone that though Protestant Ulster was to be protected against being included in Southern Ireland against its will, and though both parties had agreed in principle, no compromise could be reached. The question of whether the border villages of Fermanagh and Tyrone belonged to one side or the other was considered sufficient provocation for arms to be smuggled into

Ulster and violence encouraged by Conservative statesmen. Only the outbreak of a far more important struggle had postponed this one.

Irish Home Rule was postponed, perforce, until after the war. By 1918, the Ulster extremists had come to their senses somewhat. They accepted a separate Parliament for Ulster, and though their attitude to the border question was still intolerant, there were indications that they might perhaps under pressure from England admit a compromise. Meanwhile, Southern Ireland, which had been content with Home Rule in 1914, had now fallen under the domination of Sinn Fein extremists who demanded complete independence and control over the whole of Ireland. They set out to get it by murder of government agents, especially police. The Lloyd George government retaliated more or less in kind, with the result that an unsatisfactory, undeclared war increased the bitterness on both sides, brought the government into disrepute at home, and settled nothing. This could not go on. The British government was not prepared to compromise on two issues: the independence of Ulster and the acknowledgement by Southern Ireland that it belonged in the British Commonwealth. If therefore no concessions were to be made by Sinn Fein, there must be war.

The dramatic history of the Irish negotiations does not concern Winston Churchill very nearly. His position, however, as a Liberal with Conservative leanings did give him opportunities to sort out the issues. Some of the leading Conservative supporters of Ulster were close personal friends, while his Liberal colleagues had put Irish Home Rule on the statute book in 1914. Churchill's efforts for understanding were tireless, surprisingly so to those people who had always considered him better at picking a fight than settling a quarrel. When the representatives of Sinn Fein, belligerent and suspicious, consented to come to London to talk with representatives of the government, Churchill was present. When Michael Collins, the strong-arm man of Sinn Fein, began to lose his temper about the way he had been hunted in Ireland and a price put on his head, it was Churchill who raised a laugh by producing a Boer proclamation offering five pounds reward for the capture of Churchill, "alive or dead." Churchill's signature is on the Irish treaty together with that of Michael Collins. His interest and support encouraged the moderate Sinn Feiners to establish their rule in the face of armed uprising. His constant urging helped both sections of Ireland to take a more reasonable view when the inevitable border incidents arose. Michael Collins, who was shortly after murdered by his own extremists, sent Churchill a message. "Tell Winston we could never have done anything without him."

For his settlement of the Middle East and for the Irish treaty, Churchill deserved more credit than he received in the country. Any answer to the Irish question was bound to arouse some ill will; while the Lloyd George government by its earlier repressive measures had alienated the groups who might have supported its final agreement. Meanwhile, the soldiers who had fought to end war and make a better world were now at home, and out of work. Their government, instead of concerning itself with their plight, was settling world problems. Both in and outside Parliament there was much discontent which was waiting for an issue to crystallize. It shortly found one in the Chanak crisis.

The crisis of Chanak was very largely the fault of Lloyd George, who had permitted, if not encouraged the Greeks to make an invasion of Asia Minor, which is geographically part of the Turkish homeland, though the coast was settled by Greeks. The Turks, deprived of their empire, thrust back from the Dardanelles, were not prepared to give up any more without a struggle. Under the leadership of Mustapha Kemal, they shattered the Greeks and advanced triumphantly on the Dardanelles and Constantinople. These had been internationalized and were now guarded by a small force, consisting largely of French and British troops. The French withdrew before the Turkish advance, but the British, entrenched at Chanak, held fast. The question at issue was whether the Eastern peace settlement should be revised by armed force and in defiance of the victorious Allies. It seemed very likely that the Turks would attack Chanak and overwhelm it. What then would Britain do?

Churchill drafted and Lloyd George sent a warning communiqué which was in fact an outright threat of war. The nations of Europe held their breath. The Turks recoiled. The crisis passed. The prestige of Great Britain in the world was greatly increased, but the British people had found themselves threatening war about a quarrel which they had not understood and were not prepared for. They felt a great sense of outrage. The coalition which had held Lloyd George in power fell apart. Parliament was dissolved. An epoch was over.

By the British constitution any citizen may stand for

Parliament in any district where he has hopes of election. Churchill's constituency since 1908 had been the radical Scotch marmalade and whisky town of Dundee. Elections in Britain are lively. The candidate speaks several times every night, and he is expected to be on view all day and even to take some share in the canvassing from door to door which is carried out by his supporters.

By a sad coincidence, the night before he was off to Dundee, Churchill came down with appendicitis. Hardly was he out of the anesthetic before he wanted his secretary, no, several. He had a dozen messages which must be telephoned and numbers of people who must be summoned at once. When hospital superintendents told him about visiting hours, he said he was too busy to take any notice. When doctors protested, he pointed out his operation was their doing. All the patients who could get about a bit began to gather in the corridor outside his room, together with curious interns and people from as far away as Dundee, who were waiting to see him. Eventually he ordered a special coach on the Flying Scotsman and told his doctors he was going up to Dundee. As for the stitches which they had not yet taken out, they might leave them in there.

He left for Dundee on a stretcher six days before the election and had to be carried upstairs, in and out of halls, and onto platforms in a chair. The tide in Dundee was flowing against him, and he was not well enough to enjoy the fight, though he tried his best. Dundee was a radical town; and Winston Churchill, liberal though he might call himself, had really done nothing for the people as such since 1911. Besides, a vast change was coming over politics, a change which Churchill and his generation did not yet understand. The Labour Party, more radical, more working class than the Liberals, was about to take over. No sudden descent six days before the election, no gallant effort could alter the fact that Dundee wanted a change. Thus in a few weeks the government of Lloyd George and his party were scattered to the winds. Churchill found himself out of office and for the first time since 1901 out of Parliament altogether. After climbing the political ladder again, he was once more at the bottom.

Lady Randolph
Churchill at
about forty.

Lord Randolph
Churchill in
later life.

Hero, war correspondent, light-horse
cavalryman in South Africa, 1900.

First Lord of the Admiralty,
World War I.

A student pilot.
Punch cartoon, 1919.

The Munich Crisis, September, 1938. Churchill returning from a conference with Mr. Chamberlain, with whose policy of appeasement he does not agree.

The Atlantic Pact, 1941. Churchill and Roosevelt aboard the
Prince of Wales. Behind them are General Marshall, U. S. Army
Chief of Staff, Sumner Welles, Undersecretary of State, and
Admiral Stark, U. S. Chief of Naval Operations. Behind and to
Roosevelt's right is Churchill's personal bodyguard, Thompson.

"We shall let them have it back." Churchill visits Bristol
after a raid in April, 1941.

Costume for the Blitz. Churchill models his siren suit in Washington, January, 1942.

That nice flying boat. Churchill takes over the controls on the way back to England, January, 1942.

At a forward observation post. Churchill watches
artillery strike target area in Italy, August, 1944.

Former Naval Person. Wearing leather ear guards, Churchill watches gunnery practice aboard the battleship *Renown*, 1943.

Big three at Yalta, February, 1945.

It was time to take a real holiday. Winston Churchill and his family moved to the south of France for the next five months, where the brilliant landscapes of the Mediterranean tempted his sense of color. There was as usual much visiting and entertaining. There was swimming with much wallowing and noise. There was time for intensive thought, which was also a noisy process. From the squat figure slumped on a stool under a beach umbrella with a complex array of painting equipment beside him could be heard puffings and groanings at intervals which may have had little to do with the canvas. Getting around at his usual lumbering trot, he swung his arms while humming with about as much sense of tune as a bee. His secretaries seemed more and more unaware that this was vacation. Churchill was planning a book.

The production of a Churchillian book had become a far more complicated process than it had been in the days of the *Life of Lord Randolph Churchill*. All these years of Ministerial office had accustomed its author to working through excellent secretaries. When he wanted facts, he had them dug up. When he wanted statistics, he had them analyzed by experts instead of wasting his time poring over details. Nowadays when he tackled a book he organized it like a government department, with this only difference that

the work could not be done at the public expense. As his
fortune mounted through timely inheritances, the number
and cost of his employees also rose. He had long abandoned
the method of writing by hand. Everything was dictated
at speed, typed up, corrected, and then typed again. Meanwhile, his vast correspondence and his highly paid articles
rolled out, too. Mr. Churchill, his secretaries exclaimed,
was the most impatient of men. What he wanted, he had
to have right away. He might feel like dictating from bed;
from the bath with a half-opened door; with a towel mod-
estly draped round his middle; in shorts, undershirt, and
red cummerbund; or after midnight. And when he wanted
anything typed up immediately, he was capable of harrying
the typist to produce his manuscript complete in less than
a minute.

The World Crisis, Churchill's history of the First World
War, was barely begun on this Riviera holiday; yet it was
sufficiently planned so that during the excitement of the
months and years which followed, six volumes came out
in rapid succession. It is a remarkable book, not precisely
a history, and yet not merely the tale of Churchill's own
part in the war. It is rather the war from his own point
of view with episodes treated in detail where he happens
to have special knowledge. The second volume, which
is about the Dardanelles, is a defense of his actions which
played a large part in re-establishing his reputation. The
whole is beautifully written and fascinating in its breadth
and sweep. Mr. Balfour, as usual, had the last word. "I
have just been reading Winston's brilliant autobiography
disguised as a history of the Universe."

Amid such occupations, there was still time for thinking about politics. If Dundee did not want him, he must of course try elsewhere as soon as a chance should offer. The difficult question was, with which party ought he to be allied. The Liberal Party in their decline appeared more willing to throw in their support to the Labour Party than to their old Conservative opponents. To Churchill, the socialist doctrines of Labour seemed like communism, which he hated. Yet to join the Conservatives again after having deserted them once was not easy, in spite of the fact that he had worked with them under Lloyd George since the war and had always in some respects been Conservative at heart.

Churchill had to stand three more times for Parliament before he got in and was safely accepted inside the Conservative ranks. He was lucky in a period during which governments were weak and did not last long. Thus he was out of Parliament only about two years, during which he worked out the gradual process of changing sides in a series of campaigns against Labour. The Conservative Party was by no means entirely pleased to receive him. However, its important men were aware of his power. When he finally reappeared in Parliament, Stanley Baldwin, leader of the Party, offered him a place in the government. The story is, he had not expected this office to be important, and he was most agreeably surprised. Though the latest recruit to the Conservatives, Churchill was given the most important office which the Prime Minister has to bestow, that very office which Lord Randolph Churchill had once so briefly possessed . . . Chancellor of the Exchequer. It was a great personal triumph for Winston to stand in his father's shoes and to wear his father's robes. The Chancellor of the Exchequer has a special ceremonial robe which is usually handed on from one minister to another to save expense. Lord Randolph, however, had insisted on keeping his . . . a robe which had previously been worn by one of the greatest of England's Chancellors, old Mr. Gladstone.

Churchill was Chancellor of the Exchequer in a Conservative government from 1924 to 1929, and none of his admirers look on his record there with special pride. It was not his office, and the world of the twenties was not his world. After a period of nearly ten years of international upheaval, the pendulum had swung back to domestic affairs. The vital issues in English politics were economic; and a man who had never been able to like mathematics as a boy must be expected to find economics dreary. The task of the Chancellor is to decide what moneys must be spent and to raise them after a fashion which shall tend to increase rather than decrease prosperity. In Britain in the twenties with the burden of war debts to pay and with a vast modernization of industry necessary, too, this could not be done. Yet meanwhile, the unemployed stood at a million, about one-eighth of the labor force of the country; and neither Conservatives nor Labour could perceive how to make it much smaller.

With such enormous problems to tackle, it was a pity that Churchill did not get on better with Stanley Baldwin. Not that they quarreled, but the two were opposites. Churchill, a veteran now in politics, had personal friends but never a party. Baldwin, who had risen by sheer luck to leadership, not only united the Conservatives, but firmly established himself in the public's affections. Churchill was a fighter, and just now he was trying to fight socialism. Baldwin was more nearly an honest broker, almost an umpire. What he wanted, and indeed what he achieved was a national unity which contrasted very strangely with faction-ridden France, and which may after a fashion have won Great Britain the Second World War when France collapsed.

With these great virtues, Baldwin also combined great failings, in which he was once more the opposite of Churchill. In administration he was lazy. Far from desiring to interfere with other departments, he did not bother to inform himself when he should have done so. In Cabinet discussions, he did not always listen. When foreign affairs came up, he shut his eyes and said, "Wake me when you've finished." Churchill's ranging interests annoyed him. Indeed, he complained that Cabinet meetings could never get down to business because before they started they always had to discuss a clever memorandum which Churchill had written about someone else's department. Five years of this sort of thing was enough, and Baldwin was said to have decided that he never could work with Churchill again. In the event, he never did so.

The most important thing Churchill did during these years was restoring the gold standard and returning the value of the pound to its prewar level. He was of course advised by the experts, who told him almost with one voice that Britain's position as financial center of the world must be restored and that the measure was necessary. The fact was, even the experts did not understand the confusion of the monetary systems of the world or foresee the great depression. In 1931, the pound fell again, this time forever.

Meanwhile, the effect of Churchill's measure was felt throughout the country in widespread suffering. It had amounted to the addition of eighteen per cent to the price of every article Britain exported. Until the buying power of the pound had made itself felt by lowering the prices of imports enough to justify reduction of wages, there was bound to be more unemployment. A healthy economy might have stood the strain; but Great Britain had weaknesses already which were now to cause a great crisis.

British prosperity in the century before had been founded on her possession of plentiful and excellent coal. This she still had; but her coal mines had been developed haphazardly and before the days when mining problems were well understood. Many of them by now were uneconomic and abandoned. Many more were just on the verge of going out of business. The grim little townships which had grown up around pitheads possessed no other trade whatsoever. When the pit closed down, everybody in the town was out of work. In many cases, there never would be any work again. The people were Welsh-speaking and had small desire to migrate to somewhere in England. Nor was it easy to educate the older men to different trades.

This tragic situation was brought to a head by the rise in the price of English coal due to Churchill's measure. The mine owners' association served notice that without a drop in wages or an increase in hours of work, they must all go out of business. The miners' union, one of the

largest and best organized in the country and with a Communist leader, refused to consider either suggestion. Their
attitude was understandable, seeing that conditions of
work in the old pits were bad and that wages already were
low. Besides, the mine owners were a thoroughly selfish
group. However, at this moment the owners' backs were
really against the wall; and they were unable as well as
unwilling to cancel their demands.

This head-on clash between capital and labor in a vital
industry led by rapid transitions to an open fight between
labor and the government itself. Trade-union labor was
very conscious of power and at the same time of grievance.
The new Labour Party in Parliament had actually taken
office for a brief while with Liberal support; but because
of the Liberals it had not been able to put through drastic
measures. While mass unemployment and poor housing
conditions persisted, organized labor was in no mood to
wait for the gradual process of gaining political power.
Thus while the government sought a reorganization of the
mining industry, during which both sides would be forced
to give way somewhat, the Trades Union Council backed
the miners up with the threat of a general strike.

Such threats are easier to make than to recede from.
The T.U.C. leaders did not want to force revolution on
England, exactly, but they certainly did desire to try their
power. If they could compel the government to keep mining wages up by granting a subsidy, then there would be
no telling what they could extract from a government next.
The center of power would have moved from Parliament
to organized labor. Both sides perceived this, and on the

whole it appears the government preferred a showdown. Better tackle the problem at once if the T.U.C. could be maneuvered into putting themselves in the wrong.

Thus half desired, half feared by both sides, the General Strike took place, paralyzing industry, newspapers, transport, and in fact the whole of highly unionized Britain. It lasted ten days, during which the country visibly tottered on the edge of a revolution and spectators abroad held their breath. It was broken by the general support of the public, marshaled by the government with considerable skill — and most especially by Winston Churchill.

The important points were distribution of supplies and news. The first depended in fact upon the second, for unless the general public would co-operate wholeheartedly, no transport could be rigged up. British broadcasting was fortunately a government corporation; but though the radio was by now in countless working-class houses, the habit of listening to radio news was not universal. The government needed a newspaper as well.

The proprietor of the *Morning Post* offered his plant, and Winston Churchill immediately moved in. He had plenty to do in the Treasury, which was thrown into terrible confusion by the strike; but by rising at seven and going to bed at 3 A.M., he ran both jobs at once. There being no distributors, he called the Automobile Association for volunteers. There being no machinists, he called a submarine base for good mechanics. To find typesetters and printing experts, he called universities and trade schools for teachers or students. When windows were smashed, he got the Irish Guard. Somebody managed to throw an iron bar into the big press and sabotage it. Churchill had it hoisted out and sent down to the naval workshops of Chatham dockyard under convoy, whence it reappeared in plenty of time for the next edition.

The earliest *British Gazette* was a two-page sheet. In a week it had grown to a newspaper of eight pages with a circulation of nearly two million. There was nothing impartial about its news. In fact, it was frankly an instrument of propaganda, concerned with breaking the strike and not with presenting the whole of the picture. Socialists in Parliament were very naturally outraged, though powerless. Divided in sympathy, they felt the workers at least deserved fairer treatment. Meanwhile, the editor of the *Times* was equally angry at Churchill's perversion of the character of a free press. He wrote a memorandum for the Cabinet on the subject, but nothing was done. Churchill had made an enemy who was to do him much harm in the days to come.

The General Strike collapsed, and foreign nations were astounded at the solidarity of British public opinion. Baldwin and his colleagues settled down to legislation which they hoped would make another attempt impossible. The luckless miners stayed out for nearly six months and were starved into terms at a cost to the nation of £800,000,000 — which if invested in the industry in the first place could have solved the whole problem.

Churchill's role in the General Strike, and indeed in Baldwin's government generally, did not add much to his reputation either then or since. It certainly added nothing to his power in Conservative circles. He was gradually moving from his favorite center position out to the die-hard Tory wing, at the very moment when the general sense of the country and of the government itself inclined to the center. His unpopularity with Baldwin was certainly echoed by the rank and file of the Conservative Party. It is a moot question, however, whether he could have been kept out of power in the next Tory regime. As it happened, he solved the question himself by resigning from what is called the "shadow cabinet," in other words the inner council which the party in opposition sets up to direct its tactics.

The question over which he fell out with his colleagues was their support of the Government of India Bill in which Dominion status was recognized as being the goal of India. Churchill's objections, he being Churchill, were plausible enough. India with her caste system and her illiteracy problem would not be ready for Dominion status in foreseeable time. What she needed was an increasing share in local government. In addition, the embittered feud between Hindu and Moslem would cause massacre or civil war the moment the British had left. To give in to Gandhi on issues like these was contemptible weakness. Much of this was all very true, but the crux of the matter was not in arguments like these. The British public was absorbed in its own economic struggles and had no appetite for tackling unrest in India. It remembered Ireland and felt tired. Winston Churchill never was tired, while his attitude to the Empire was basically an emotional one. He looked upon England as the great civilizer of peoples. It was her inheritance to rule, and he would uphold it.

Thus Churchill drew away from the Conservatives once more, but this time there was nowhere else to go. Liberalism was dead, socialism not for him. He was out of sympathy with Baldwin's policy of plodding along and not facing issues until they had to be faced, yet he had to remain in the party. There was nothing for it but to become a Conservative lone wolf and waste his energies on criticism without the power to be constructive. Never before had he stood more completely outside the main current of public life. He was now in his middle fifties, not too old to do good work, yet compelled to perceive that time was drifting past him. Somehow or other he had never quite come off, except as a writer. He was starting another ambitious work, this time a justification and a biography of his famous ancestor, the Duke of Marlborough, who had saved Europe from the domination of France under Louis XIV.

It was in the 1920's after *The World Crisis* and several legacies had established him as a fairly wealthy man that Churchill bought as his permanent home the manor of Chartwell. It suited him exactly, not as it stood, but as a point of departure, as something he could remodel without spoiling. It was near enough to London so that people could drive down to lunch or dinner. Accommodation was adequate for his Parliamentary secretary, shorthand typists, research assistants, maids, valet, and family, not to mention a friend or two and a specialist called into consultation about some project which he might have in mind. The house was dignified with age, and yet not gloomy. His own particular bedroom-cum-study was a vast and sunny room with a cathedral ceiling, fine oak beams, and view of water.

There was a lake and a pond, both quite small and easy to interfere with. Besides, the original grounds were not sufficiently large. When extra lots had been added, there must be grading, several acres of perfect lawn, and hedges planted. Winston Churchill, who did not now play polo any more and only occasionally took exercise on horseback, was getting plump and pink. He took to manual labor with joy. It was not that he contemplated reconstructing the grounds of Chartwell with his own hands. Far from it. But having assembled an army of gardeners, brick-layers, masons, and so forth, he was unable to stand about and watch without joining in. He then discovered how much he liked wheeling heavy barrows or changing the face of nature in a perfectly visible way. In particular, he wanted to play with that water.

He started by damming the brook which fed his little lake, and thus making another little lake which filled up fast. Next, he wanted a swimming pool. Churchill was a dangerous man to stay with or work for in periods like these. Every male was pressed into helping him dig or line his pool, which when finished was too cold to swim in. This gave Churchill a chance to devise an ingenious system of feeding it warmer water. Other people with poor circulation or less natural padding still tended to leave it alone. Winston, however, put up a diving board and had many a wallow, displacing a vast amount of water with his powerful trudgeon. He was not satisfied with this achievement because the brook which flowed out the far end of his pool was simply wasted. He constructed a goldfish pond below, and fed its inhabitants so faithfully over the years that they grew to enormous size and would swim hopefully up to the side as soon as he appeared.

In the midst of these occupations, he discovered another hobby. There was a fair amount of brickwork needed on the estate; new walls, and various cottages to be repaired. Bricklaying is a reasonably skilled art involving some heavy labor and the joys of mixing cement. Unluckily the brick-layers' union frowned upon amateur helpers. Churchill decided to join the union himself and pay his dues. The local officials could produce no good reason why not, but the general council of the trade were outraged. Winston Churchill, the man who ran the *British Gazette,* the die-hard enemy of socialism! Angrily they demanded that he resign. Impressively Churchill replied that he was a perfectly good bricklayer, and in a position to prove it. Majestically he complained that to drag in his "incidental duties" as Chancellor of the Exchequer was begging the question. Crushingly he added they were merely insulting the dignity of organized skilled labor in the person of one of its members. The union found itself helpless, while Churchill, having discovered a creative job which he liked, went on laying bricks.

He had taken time off in 1931 for a profitable lecture tour of the United States, accompanied only by his wife and daughter, an indispensable secretary, and a bodyguard in case of Indian terrorists. However, the dangers of New York proved different from expectation. Hardly had he and his party been whirled off the boat to the Waldorf Astoria by the sirens of a police escort than Mr. Churchill decided to go out at once and see Bernard Baruch. Forgetting that in America traffic keeps to the right, he darted out into Fifth Avenue with one of his impulsive lunges and was knocked down by a taxi. He ought to have been killed, but with his usual luck he got off with deep lacerations of the head and chest and a sprained right shoulder. He spent several days in the Lenox Hill Hospital, collecting enough flowers to supply almost every patient in the place and dictating an article for *Collier's* about how it felt to be knocked down which brought him in enough money to take three weeks' recuperation in the Bahamas before going on tour. After this, he worked his shattering way across the country, upsetting the peaceful routine of America's best hotels for three months and a half, while addressing audiences which averaged over four thousand.

It was at Chartwell during the early thirties that Churchill began his four-volume life of Marlborough. The Labour government which had turned Baldwin out in 1929 had lasted only until the full effect of the world depression hit Great Britain. In the moment of crisis, a national government was formed in which Ramsay MacDonald, the Labour leader, remained Prime Minister, but power passed into the hands of Stanley Baldwin. Churchill was not asked to join what was more or less a Conservative government in disguise. He remained a mere member of Parliament without much power or policy, except a negative one in the case of India. In other words, apart from the work and organization needed to produce the great Marlborough volumes, he had time on his hands for a new enterprise.

In the summer of 1932, he was traveling in Europe for the purpose of tracing Marlborough's great campaigns in the lands of the Rhine and the Danube. He was making a leisurely trip with his family and usual entourage while exercising that masterly eye for terrain and memory for detail which was later to confound professional guides on the field of Gettysburg. However, while studying the history of the past he was never unaware of the present. In fact, he was very much struck by the ferment in the country over Hitler.

It was the fashion in England at about that time to shrug

off Hitler as a weird extremist thrown up by the depression who would as times improved lose influence. Indeed, the peak of his movement, as people thought, was already past. But no one who was actually in Germany in 1932 could have imagined that such vast political frenzy would disappear without trace. Churchill was clearly startled. Knowing little about Hitler or his program, he found himself anxious to know more. As it happened, the course of his wanderings led him to Munich, Hitler's headquarters. At the hotel, a favorite of Hitler's called Hanfstaengl struck up an acquaintance, was asked to dinner, and entertained the party by playing and singing. Churchill had a passion for a nice, catchy tune with a good rum-te-tum, and his repertory was large as a result of faithful attendance at musical comedy over the years. He and Hanfstaengl had an excellent evening, during which Hanfstaengl suggested a meeting with Hitler, which he could easily arrange. Churchill was willing, even anxious, but he spoiled his chances by letting slip his personal opinion of the nonsense that Hitler was talking about the Jews. As a result Hitler, who had apparently inspired the whole contact, backed out. Two national leaders who were to hear much of each other in the future failed to meet.

Churchill came back from Germany in a thoughtful mood. Six months later when Hitler seized power in a sudden coup and when the persecution of political foes and Jews began, he was increasingly disturbed. The steps which were being taken to build up German military strength were most alarming. Unluckily the present British government was largely concerned with careful finance. It had been set up to restore national credit after the great depression, and as a result it was happy to economize on armaments, which are expensive. Stanley Baldwin, in so far as he had thoughts on foreign affairs, did not lack sound horse sense. He did not, however, dare to give a strong lead to the country because he was alarmed by the strength of pacifist feeling and afraid of losing his popularity. Ramsay MacDonald, the nominal Prime Minister, had been a pacifist throughout the First World War and combined a considerable shrewdness in matters he understood with the vaguest, woolliest moral convictions on those he did not. Meanwhile, the Labour Party as a whole, which formed the Opposition, was strongly anti-war. In consequence, upon neither side of the political fence was there any willingness to look awkward facts in the face or take necessary action.

It was in these unpromising circumstances that Churchill found himself back more or less at Agadir. History repeats itself, but with a difference. The militarist empire was once more taking shape, and the man who had met its first challenge was once more aware. This time, however, he had no government or nation behind him. Almost alone he confronted a far more aggressive tyrant than the Kaiser, and one more determined on war. The most Churchill could hope for was a very small group of supporters in Parliament, plus the minor resources he could personally muster at Chartwell. He set himself to make the best of both.

The Parliamentary group which Churchill collected on the question of national defense contained some important names and could insist on being heard. Meanwhile at Chartwell regular information from the Foreign Office, the French general staff, newspaper correspondents, and distinguished opponents of Hitler were compared. Churchill's contacts had always been enormously wide, and his elaborate organization now turned itself into a miniature Foreign Office which by concentrating on the subject of Germany became very well informed.

Meanwhile, the tragedy of Europe developed at a steady pace. Mr. MacDonald pressed disarmament on France and advocated an equal allowance of military strength for the Germans. The British public tended to think this fair and shut its eyes to the danger of allowing Germany to rearm when in the power of a regime which was openly bent on making trouble. Long-drawn-out discussions which ended in failure gave Hitler time to start preliminary training in his labor camps and private "army," and above all to set up machinery for the construction of an air force.

It was on the German air force that Churchill's attention was chiefly fastened. By the Treaty of Versailles after World War I, Germany had been forbidden military aircraft. However, secret plans had long been drawn up for converting private factories to military production. This was now being done at speed, while preliminary training was being given to pilots through glider clubs. By every ingenious method, Hitler was pushing the construction of a formidable air force. Great Britain, though very vulnerable to air attack and possessed only of the fifth air force in the world, could easily have kept her lead, had she taken alarm. Yet when in the middle of 1934 the government inoffensively and with apologies put forward proposals for a modest increase of about eight hundred machines over the next five years, the Labour opposition, greatly though it hated the Nazis, did not fail to raise the cry of "warmongers." It was left to Churchill to state from the information in his possession that Germany was already two-thirds as strong as Britain in the air and by the end of 1935 would be nearly equal. In November of the same year he repeated this estimate, and Mr. Baldwin got up to contradict his figures. By the end of 1935, Mr. Baldwin said, at the present rate of progress, the British air force would still be one and one-half times the German.

Everyone was much reassured to find that Mr. Churchill as usual was dramatizing. The government with its excellent sources of information must know the figures. Indeed, it was the government's duty to know them. In any case, as the papers emphasized, Mr. Baldwin had promised to see that England always kept safely ahead.

The public went back to sleep. But Hitler himself was not disposed to keep his power a secret. Less than six months later, in March of 1935, he felt strong enough to inform the Foreign Secretary that Germany's air force was already as large as Great Britain's. Mr. Baldwin had to admit in Parliament that he had been quite wrong and to accept responsibility for Britain's danger.

Amazingly enough, this extraordinary episode actually strengthened Baldwin's hand rather than Churchill's. The Labour Party, hoping to fight the coming election on anti-war slogans, hardly liked to take the matter up. The Liberals, probably also with the election in mind, charged off at a tangent to attack private munitions firms. Meanwhile, the Conservatives actually liked Baldwin better for being, as they said, courageous enough to admit when he was mistaken. Uneasiness merely caused them to solidify their ranks and to talk of taking precautions. Hurricanes and Spitfires, which were already on the designing board, were now to be put into production. But as no one ventured to squander the nation's carefully gathered resources, Germany drew ahead.

The truth was, not only the politicians, but the nation itself had little patience with Churchill. His political gospel was that eternal truth of British politics, the balance of European power. Once let that balance be upset by German domination, and Britain must be endangered along with France and all the smaller nations on Germany's eastern border. This conception was felt to be cynical and out of date. Had not half the wars in British history been fought to preserve the balance of power? The League of Nations had superseded all that and was the only possible answer to war, particularly in Europe.

Neither Churchill nor Baldwin understood the idealism of the people about the League of Nations, since neither had any illusions about the League's real strength. In this very same year, Mussolini decided to conquer a fellow member of the League, Abyssinia; but neither British statesman was entirely prepared to take the lead against him. In Churchill's view, British interests in Europe depended on France. By 1935 France was in no position to quarrel with Italy, lest Germany seize the same moment for action against her. Britain should therefore hang back and not force France into awkward decisions.

The Baldwin government, on the other hand, made the mistake of playing two policies at once, one popular and the other realistic. It stood forth in the League as champion of the oppressed and rallied its nations to impose embargoes on war materials going to Italy. Perceiving, however, that Mussolini meant business and would declare war on the British if they closed Suez or cut off vital supplies such as oil, Baldwin did nothing drastic. Moreover, after winning the election by a large majority because of its courageous stand, the government turned around to join with France in making a deal whereby Mussolini was to be given a large part of Abyssinia to stop him fighting.

This abrupt return to power politics outraged the people to such an extent that though the government possessed an enormous majority in Parliament, it was unable to resist the popular fury. The Foreign Secretary who had made the agreement with Italy was removed. Baldwin apologized and went back to embargoes, which were just enough to earn Mussolini's undying enmity, and yet not adequate to prevent him from swallowing the whole of Abyssinia. Moreover, perceiving that Britain and France dared not act effectively, Hitler took a chance; and though his forces were not ready, he reoccupied the Rhineland.

Hitler's gamble came off. France and England did nothing. The scales of power, which had been trembling for some time, came down with a thud in the German direction. Ever since the peace treaty, this German borderland had been a demilitarized zone. By occupying it with troops and building fortifications opposite the French Maginot Line, Hitler could put himself in a position to do what he pleased in Europe. For if he desired to invade France, he could always as in 1914 tear up the treaties and make his attack through Belgium, where the French frontier was still unfortified. If on the other hand he wished to employ his forces in Eastern Europe, he could stand on the defensive against France on an immensely strong line. There was no question of France ever tearing up the Belgian treaty. Thus Germany gained a free hand in the east against Austria, Czechoslovakia, and Poland; while Mussolini, who had so far protected Austria, was too angry with the Western Powers to do so any longer.

All these tremendous events alarmed the British, who had had the worst of both Baldwin policies: making an enemy of Italy, while yet allowing the authority of the League to be set at nothing. Naturally Churchill's warnings, little heeded until now, were gaining importance. The government spoke of faster rearmament and a minister to co-ordinate defense. Many people, including Churchill himself, felt he was the man for this job. However, Baldwin was reluctant to work with Churchill again; and considering the majority which he still had in the House, he did not need to. The co-ordination of defense went to an obscure lawyer with no experience of this sort and no sign of ability for it. Churchill had to be content with a place on the Committee for Air Defence Research, in which he gained invaluable knowledge of the latest scientific developments, particularly radar.

Churchill was angry. He did not know at the time how lucky he was to have no share in the blame for British policy during these years. Very naturally his anger lent sharpness to his attack on the government's halfhearted organization. It also allowed Parliament to suppose that his real purpose was to get office. People still remembered how he had crossed to the Liberals in 1906 and been rewarded by the Under-Secretaryship of the Colonies, how he had returned in 1924 and again been rewarded by the Chancellorship of the Exchequer. It was easy to put down his present agitation to nothing but pressure on the government to take him in. The elaborate rhetoric he used was out of style. People enjoyed it, and yet they followed the fashion of thinking that a simpler form of speech was more sincere.

In spite of these drawbacks, Churchill's reputation was bound to grow, if only as a prophet of doom. Indeed, it seemed merely a question of time until the Baldwin government would be forced against its will to take him in. But in 1936, another sort of crisis in which Churchill took the unpopular side destroyed his chances.

The desire of King Edward VIII to marry Mrs. Ernest Simpson was unfortunately timed amid these emergencies. With war menacing Europe, this was no moment to strain the bonds of Empire or trouble the allegiance of the Dominions to the British crown. Accordingly, Mr. Baldwin laid before the King the straight alternatives of giving up the crown or giving up the lady. Edward, who naturally would have liked a compromise, wished to consult with somebody outside the government; and he picked upon Churchill as a very old acquaintance and the most distinguished man in such a position.

Churchill's loyalty was both deep and emotional. When a young man, he had been troubled for a while by being unable to reconcile intellectual views with religion. He had solved this problem in a perfectly illogical way by simply deciding to believe whatever he felt was worth believing. By a similar process, he was the devoted subject of the monarchy. It was the colorful center of centuries of British history, and he valued great traditions more than exact logic. When, therefore, he was appealed to by his King, he felt it his duty not only to give advice, but to speak up in Parliament on the King's behalf. However, the government, and indeed the Parliament as a whole, was more concerned with its own difficulties in this matter of Mrs. Simpson than with the King's. On this issue it was possible that the whole country, indeed the whole empire might become deeply divided. If Edward himself or if Churchill were to rally the country, there was little doubt that the people would have split into factions. Those who already suspected Churchill of vulgar ambition were aware that this situation was made for an unscrupulous agitator. Sure enough, Churchill got up to speak for the King. It mattered little that what he said was no more than a plea for delay and for Parliamentary discussion. Both were dangerous in view of the feeling of the people and the crisis in Europe. The unanimous opinion of Parliament was against Churchill. He found himself eventually shouted down in a demonstration of anger which few private members of the House ever attracted. Everybody's worst suspicions of his character and motives seemed confirmed.

Mr. Baldwin retired some six months later after the

coronation of King George VI, and once more the offices of the government were shuffled around. The new Prime Minister, Neville Chamberlain, was one of a distinguished political family and had won a great reputation for efficiency and hard work. He had in fact been the driving force behind Baldwin. It was he who had re-established Great Britain's financial credit in the early thirties. His relations with Churchill were far from intimate. They were colored in part by the fact that Chamberlain detested Lloyd George, in part by the general prejudice against Churchill inside the party, and certainly in part by the lack of sympathy which a shy, retiring man often feels for a confident, loud one. At all events, it is significant that after nearly twenty years together in Parliament, during most of which they had both been prominent members of the same party organization, their personal contacts were limited to casual words on formal occasions.

It was hardly to be expected that Neville Chamberlain would be willing to take Churchill into his government. His personal attitude might have been overcome, but his views on policy, which were far more active than Baldwin's had been, were the opposite of Churchill's. It is true that both men agreed that British rearmament was the urgent need of the hour. Their only difference in this particular respect was in degree. Chamberlain was a businessman and a financier. Extravagance went against the grain, and all his instincts forbade him to interfere with peacetime trade. Nor was he a very good chooser of men or easy to work for. However, much was put in hand, and there was no question that by 1940 or 1941 the flow of munitions should be considerable. Even Churchill allowed that his attitude toward the new government was almost avuncular . . . not fatherly, he was in haste to add, since a child of his getting would certainly be bolder and brisker. All the same, progress was being made in the right direction. This was, however, still 1937. How could Great Britain get through the next few years until her strength came back?

It was on this point that Neville Chamberlain had fresh views. The dictators, and Hitler in especial, were people with a grievance. Remove their grievance, and they must inevitably simmer down. Nor was it reasonable that Britain, glutted with the victories of many wars, should always claim to have everything while others had nothing. Chamberlain was prepared to make very large concessions over a few years at least. He wanted, moreover, to make personal contacts with Hitler and Mussolini. His reasoning here appears to have been that dictators are vain and are not accustomed to deal with subordinates. They need to be flattered. He did not promise himself enjoyment in his task, since men with a grievance are apt to indulge themselves by being rude; but in the interests of his country and of the world, he would have patience.

Thus Chamberlain set out to reach understanding with the dictators through concessions. There is an ancient proverb which he might well have called to mind, "Who sups with the devil must have a long spoon." For he did not have a long spoon. His very appearance was against him. Upright and slender in spite of advancing years, he had regular features, dark eyes, hair white at the temples as though he had dabbed it with powder, and elsewhere iron-gray. But what might have been good looks were spoiled by a very small head and a neck too long and scrawny, giving him the appearance of an inoffensive old bird. His costume, rigidly formal with stiff collar and tightly rolled umbrella, was to look absurdly old-fashioned in the lands of the jackboot and the outsized military headgear. It represented, moreover, a real rigidity of mind. There being no devils in his ordinary world, he did not understand Hitler. It does not seem to have occurred to him that Hitler did not want to forego a grievance and could not afford to simmer down. The German dictator had committed his country's finances to such an extent that he must recoup them by plunder or in the end go bankrupt. Besides, his ambitions were of such a world-wide sort that no gentlemanly offer of a battleship or a colony or two could quiet him. Naturally both he and Mussolini took what they could get, but they utterly despised the weakness which they assumed had prompted the offer. Here, too, they mistook their man. In spite of appearances, Chamberlain was not a weakling.

This appeasement policy was of all things most calculated to outrage Winston Churchill. It had always been his contention that the time to make concessions is the time when one is strong. In the early thirties, before Germany had matched Britain and France, he had suggested fresh examination of the trouble spots of Europe. Then was the moment to remove past grievances and smooth the future. Now a bold front and a steadfast policy could alone make Britain respected and might possibly win her a breathing space. Indeed, this had always been true.

Churchill had never contented himself with merely urging that Britain hasten to rearm. She should in addition have forced the Germans to conform more or less to the Versailles Treaty. She should have thrown Hitler out of the Rhineland, never allowed him to start rebuilding his fleet, and put on pressure to prevent him from reintroducing conscription. All these causes were now lost, but Britain's danger could only be increased by losing more.

The position of a prophet of evil is bound to be at its most poignant just before the great storm breaks, when little can be done. It was in Churchill's nature to face the worst unterrified, yet even his massive character was deeply stirred. He tells us how when Chamberlain took over negotiations with Italy, Eden, the Foreign Secretary and an enemy to appeasement, resigned. At this departure of the only man in the government advocating a more vigorous foreign policy, sleep forsook Churchill for the first time in years, perhaps for the only time in his life when much was endured. "I watched the daylight slowly creep in through the windows, and saw before me in mental gaze the vision of Death." [1]

Death was not long in making an appearance. Within a month, Hitler had annexed Austria. Within two, he was fomenting trouble in the border lands of Czechoslovakia, now partly surrounded on the south and on the west by the new German frontier. Czechoslovakia had been a creation of the Treaty of Versailles, which gave independence to several races long ruled by the Austro-Hungarian Empire.

[1] Winston S. Churchill, *The Gathering Storm*. Boston: Houghton Mifflin Co., 1948.

Naturally the splitting of such an old unity had caused problems. If Czechoslovakia was to be an economic and geographic whole, capable of a separate existence, it must include a German-speaking border zone. These Sudeten Germans were now encouraged to provoke racial clashes and to complain of persecution. Very clearly, in a short time Hitler would intervene to "protect" them.

The welfare of the small countries created in Eastern Europe by the Treaty of Versailles had always been of special interest to France, who saw in them a make-weight against the power of Germany or, if need arose, a buffer against Soviet Russia. France, accordingly, had long had a treaty with Czechoslovakia binding her to defend that country in war. Britain, however, had no such thing; and Chamberlain was determined not to sign one. Even though Russia showed her agitation about the threat to Eastern Europe, Chamberlain was not encouraged to do more than put pressure on the Czechs to conciliate Hitler.

The Czech crisis deepened through the summer of 1938, while Hitler made his preparations and assured himself that France and Britain would not fight. This was to be the biggest German operation so far, since the Czech border was strongly fortified. Besides, the Czech army was nearly a million and a half and well supplied by Skoda, the second biggest munitions firm in Central Europe. Not that a conflict between the two countries would ever be in doubt, but a temporary setback would damage Hitler's prestige and might encourage France, Russia, or England to join in the war. Hitler's generals were nervous, but he himself was confident — and with reason. France was pri-

vately inquiring whether if she went to war for Czechoslovakia, Britain would follow. The Chamberlain government, talking vaguely of the Empire and the Dominions,
was putting France off.

By the middle of September, the crucial stage was
reached. The leader of the Sudeten Germans fled to Hitler.
Negotiations with the Czechs were broken off. The argument was ready to move on from the question of how the
German minority could be protected inside Czechoslovakia.
Mr. Chamberlain, pursuing his policy of personal contact,
flew to meet Hitler and was confronted by his demand for
outright annexation of the German districts. He flew back
home to consult with the French, who had by now decided not to honor the word of France by fighting for
Czechoslovakia. Pressure was accordingly put on the
Czechs by Britain and France to agree to German demands.
Mr. Chamberlain, however, flying back to Hitler with these
concessions in his hand, was there confronted by a whole
set of new demands more outrageous than ever. Convinced
though he really was by Hitler's assurance that the Czech
question was the last German grievance in Europe, this
treatment was more than Chamberlain could swallow. He
returned to Great Britain, where with the Cabinet he rejected the German terms, deciding at last to fight for the
Czechs.

The ultimate moment had arrived. Most reluctantly the
French army was partly mobilized. Orders went out to
the British fleet. In preparation for the unknown horrors
of air war, men were digging trenches in the London parks
and giving out gas masks. Winston Churchill, who would

certainly be needed in case of war, was in communication with the Prime Minister and the Foreign Office, pressing for a declaration that France and England in this would act with Russia. Only to a solid determined front, he repeated, would Germany yield.

Chamberlain, however, was still alert for a chance of appeasement. He had sent a personal letter to Hitler; and the reply he had received seemed vaguely to promise that there might be an opening for compromise. Meanwhile, the French, even less eager than the British, were putting forward a compromise of their own. In consequence, Hitler condescended to put off war for another twenty-four hours while the Prime Ministers of Britain and France met with himself and Mussolini for a last-minute conference at Munich. Neither the Russians, who had been most willing to take a firm line, nor the Czechs, whose fate was at issue, were invited.

Chamberlain returned from Munich with an agreement to cut a large section off Czechoslovakia and transfer it to Hitler. He was also waving a paper which Hitler had signed at his request, declaring that the peoples of Germany and England did not ever intend to go to war. To the cheering crowds which surrounded his house in Downing Street, he spoke from the balcony, using the phrases, ". . . peace with honor. I believe it is peace in our time."

The people of England accepted the Munich agreement with huge relief. Few of them had emotional ties with Czechoslovakia, and the very existence of a German minority there had until a few months ago been unsuspected. The English had been resigned to fight if they must, but they were not eager. Amid general rejoicing, the terms of the Munich agreement were hardly examined, nor were the issues understood. These were, however, quite simple. As Mr. Churchill so neatly put it in Parliament, "We have sustained a total and unmitigated defeat, and France has suffered even more than we have . . . One pound was demanded at the pistol's point. When it was given, two pounds were demanded at the pistol's point. Finally the Dictator consented to take £1 17s. 6d., and the rest in promises of good will for the future . . . the whole equilibrium of Europe has been deranged, and . . . the terrible words have for the time being been pronounced against the Western Democracies: 'Thou art weighed in the balance and found wanting.'" [2]

As the truth of these unkind remarks penetrated to people more aware of the issue involved, their violence of feeling rocked ancient friendships or party ties and shook the Cabinet. One minister had resigned. The rest put up with what they could not alter, emphasizing that Britain was unprepared for war. Those Conservative members who joined Churchill in opposing the Munich agreement were now more than ever a small group apart, while the majority stood angrily on the defensive. Even Churchill's own safe constituency, which had returned him to Parliament since 1924, muttered against him, causing him to threaten that he would resign and fight a new election. But events were to justify him swiftly. For it was true that the balance of power in Europe was fundamental to Eng-

[2] *The Gathering Storm.*

land. The British people, who had been so unenthusias-
tically ready to fight for Czechoslovakia, were soon to discover that they must fight, no matter what the cause, or
suffer Hitler to expand across the whole of Eastern Europe. Czechoslovakia, deprived of her fortress line and
means of defense, dragged on her precarious existence only
till March. Then Hitler, who had emphasized at Munich
that he had no designs on those of non-German blood, took
over the country in cynical disregard of his signature not
six months dry on the Munich Treaty.

Neville Chamberlain was an honest man, a patriot, and
no coward. It was now revealed to him that Hitler meant
deliberate mischief. Already Germany was beginning to
foment race troubles in Poland. Not three weeks after
Hitler's march into Czechoslovakia, Chamberlain announced he had given to Poland the guarantee which
Czechoslovakia had sought in vain. If Hitler attempted to
march into Poland, His Majesty's Government had agreed
it would declare war. Too late Chamberlain did his best
to create a nucleus of friendly states extending from the
Baltic through southern Europe to Turkey. Unluckily his
change of heart did not apply to Russia, whom Poland
and other border states feared equally with the Germans.
Talks were commenced, but too late, though Churchill
constantly urged them. They dragged on too long without
issue. Eventually Russia decided to deal with the Germans
instead of the West.

Meanwhile in England conscription was introduced for
the first time during peace. It was quite generally accepted
that there must soon be war. Nobody defended the Munich

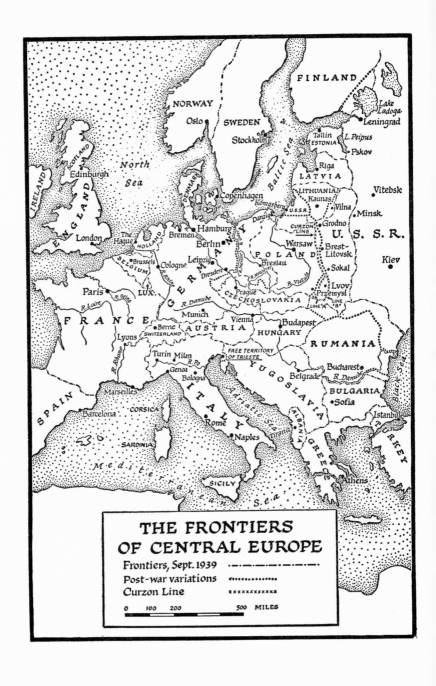

THE FRONTIERS
OF CENTRAL EUROPE

Frontiers, Sept. 1939	–·–·–·–·–·–
Post-war variations	••••••••••••
Curzon Line	××××××××××

0   100   200   500   MILES

agreement, save in terms of having won England more time to rearm. The modernization of the air force was actually gaining ground on that of the Germans. During this period, Churchill found himself at long last the man of the hour. People pressed him on the unwilling Chamberlain. Huge posters appeared saying, "Churchill must come back." Chamberlain, however, still delayed, still suspicious of Churchill's personality, or hoping for peace. So conspicuous had Churchill grown in the eyes of the world that to take him into the government now would amount to deciding on war.

War came in early September. On the first of the month, Hitler invaded Poland. Within a few hours, Chamberlain had offered Churchill a place on the War Cabinet. Details, however, must wait until the country was formally at war. In this there was a delay, due largely to the French, who wished to complete the first stages of their mobilization unhindered. However, it was significant of a great change that Parliament jumped to the conclusion that Chamberlain was looking for a way out and might yet betray Poland. In the evening of September 2nd, before a packed House, Mr. Chamberlain delivered a vague, inconclusive statement. It was received in shocked silence. After a moment, Arthur Greenwood got up to speak for the Labour opposition. As he did so, Leopold Amery, one of Labour's right-wing foes, jumped up and shouted to his opponent, "Speak for England!" And the House cheered.

Chamberlain, however, did mean business, as events proved. On the Sunday, September third, England was at war. It was now agreed that Churchill should have the

Admiralty. Some of his supporters were grieved that he had been given a department at all, since they really desired and expected him to run the whole war. Churchill, however, was anxious to have a definite task; and of course the Admiralty would have been his particular choice. There was no time to be wasted waiting for the formalities which go with the transfer of office. He took over at six o'clock, walked into the Admiralty by the old, familiar way, seated himself in the identical chair which had been waiting for this moment since 1915. Meanwhile the Admiralty, which had not forgotten one of its greatest First Lords, had sent out to the Fleet a simple message of vast significance for England: "Winston is back."

In the high, Gothic hall of the House of Commons, members' comfort is sacrificed to their debating convenience. Since many members will not be present on most occasions, it follows that either much must be said to half-filled benches, or else when matters of great moment come up, there will not be room. Accordingly, on May 7th, 1940, the House was packed like a tin of sardines, with members sitting sideways, half on and half off a bench, or standing in the doorways. Earnest, well-meaning persons, elected in a time of peace on an issue long forgotten, put up with these cramped positions rather quietly. Each was wrestling with his private fears and worries, eying dubiously Mr. Chamberlain on the Treasury bench, while the odd, squat, dwarfish figure of Leopold Amery tore into shreds the government's record.

Amery was an older man, a schoolfellow of Winston's. He had behind him nearly thirty years of Parliament and a position by no means undistinguished; but very possibly this was his greatest day. The Conservative Party had entered the war in the previous September with a clear majority of over two hundred. Its natural reaction had been to unite behind its leader in the national crisis. Mr. Chamberlain had announced that Britain was at war with almost too much emotion, laying emphasis on his own disappointed hopes and the terrible manner in which the whole purpose of his life was laid in ruin. Nevertheless, he had been visibly determined. Both sections of his party, those who had followed himself and those who had supported Churchill, were now at last in agreement. Even the Opposition, though refusing to join an all-party government, was prepared to back Chamberlain to the hilt. The voice of England spoke unanimously for war.

It was now eight months later. All the harmony which common purpose had produced was scattered to the winds. Amery represented a Conservative group containing such distinguished figures as Sir Roger Keyes, who had previously spoken in his uniform of Admiral of the Fleet to lend his professional weight to criticism of the recent campaign in Norway. Amery had begun his attack by echoing this. "Wars are won," he pointed out, "not by explanation after the event, but by foresight, by clear decision and by swift action. I confess I did not feel there was one sentence in the Prime Minister's speech this afternoon which suggested that the Government either foresaw what Germany meant to do, or came to a clear decision when it knew what Germany had done." These were strong words, especially since Liberal and Labour leaders were only waiting their turn to underline them. Members listened in a worried, angry mood, while Amery went on to comment on the Chancellor's statement that Britain's war effort would only increase by ten per cent in the next year's time. Nobody was saying as yet, but some were thinking that Britain was losing the war under her present leadership. Yet the responsibility for holding together in times of trial weighed upon all.

The 1939 war had held as many surprises for the public as the earlier one, but of an opposite sort. For nothing had happened. The German forces were away on their eastern frontier devouring Poland. In the west, they stood on the defensive in the fortified Rhineland. The French, less numerous than the Germans and bled white in the First World War, stood on the defensive likewise on their Maginot Line. They also grumbled with some justice about the inadequate size of Britain's army. They objected to British air raids over Germany, except for the purpose of scattering leaflets, pointing out that France would suffer from German reprisals. Indeed, the general notion of the French seemed to be that it was wiser not to provoke the Germans at all. Thus as the winter wore on, American news correspondents, disappointed and dull, wrote home about the "phony war." This apt piece of rudeness played its own small part in annoying those of the British who had been drafted and found no equipment ready, or who had offered their know-how to the government and been told, "Not just at present." The British machine, so its government said, was getting into gear; and the question of whether it was doing so at speed was hard to determine. Most people had their little doubts, but stuck to their leaders.

While the land war proved frustrating, the war at sea under Winston Churchill was less so. The British people were not so naïve about sea war as in 1914. The grim realities of blockade, mines, submarines, or riding herd on convoys bulked larger in their minds than the hope of sea battles or the nuisance of raiders. Naturally they feted the men who defeated the *Graf Spee;* but when the battleship *Royal Oak* was torpedoed at anchor in Scapa Flow by a German submarine, they set up no cry for a scapegoat, recognizing that such disasters would be efficiently dealt with. Meantime, the prompt recognition of the magnetic mine and its conquest was understood as a victory of no mean sort to the Admiralty's credit. Churchill's stock rose steadily through the opening months of the war; and this was true not only with the public, but in the government as his vast experience and initiative made itself felt.

But while the British and French did nothing, others had acted. The Russians, in process of enlarging their borders to cope with a possible German attack, invaded Finland. Little Finland, resisting with the utmost gallantry, drew on itself the eyes of Europe. Plenty of well-meaning people were innocently ready to take on the Russians and Germans at once if the cause were good; and the British were only prevented from sending help to the Finns by the fact that Sweden and Norway persisted in refusing to allow the passage of troops. These two Scandinavian countries were the source of Germany's iron ore, which was shipped across the Baltic in summer, but which in winter crept down the Norwegian coast inside territorial waters, yet in full view and reach of British patrol ships. Thus it was that for two reasons the Chamberlain government was debating how to put a little pressure on Norway without risking anything thereby; for it was not willing to spoil the purity of its cause by appearing to bully. Hesitating thus and arguing each move with the French, Britain was again caught by surprise. Hitler too had perceived the importance of Norway; but he had made a decision and prepared to act. Early in the spring he invaded Norway, about a week after Chamberlain, congratulating the British on an undisturbed winter of preparation, had used an unlucky phrase, "Hitler has missed the bus."

The British people were violently stirred by the invasion of Norway. The long Norwegian coastline was more convenient to their island than it was to Germany. Besides, an expedition across high seas under the nose of their fleet was an impudence. Churchill promised them vengeance. People were delighted that the Germans had moved out into the open where one could get at them.

It was now the seventh of May, and Parliament had assembled to hear the government explain its failure in Norway. Hitler had won with contemptuous ease, though most of his warships had been either damaged or destroyed. The position at the moment was that with the exception of Narvik, a tiny northern port, no place in Norway was in Allied hands or likely to become so. It was in these circumstances that Amery chose to lift the debate above temporary issues by making a violent attack against the government's very existence, pronouncing against it famous and scornful words with which the dictator Cromwell had dismissed a Parliament which showed no sign of ever dissolving. "You have sat too long here for any good you have been doing. Depart, I say. Let us have done with you. In the name of God, go!"

Strangely enough, Chamberlain had not made a bad case

for himself. The Norway fiasco as such was hardly his fault. Besides, it had chiefly been due to a failure in air power which went back to 1934 and was blamable on Baldwin. But the House had lost its patience. Many were looking not for a good excuse, but for a change in leaders. Duff Cooper, continuing the debate on the following day, was to characterize the whole of Chamberlain's administration as a series of reverses: Hitler's march into Austria, his mobilization against the Czechs, his breach of the Munich agreement, his attacks on Poland and Norway. Time and time again the House had been recalled, "always to record a setback, a disaster, always to listen to the disappointment, the astonishment, and the surprise of the Prime Minister." Decidedly the time had gone by for the best of excuses.

In this remarkable debate, not the least obvious thing was the effort which most of the speakers made to spare Winston Churchill. He was as responsible as any man in the Cabinet for the loss of the Norwegian campaign, seeing that the Navy had been the chief weapon in Britain's hand. Angrily he said so. But Lloyd George, who was making his last great contribution to his country's welfare, swiftly retorted, "The Right Honourable Gentleman must not allow himself to be converted into an air-raid shelter to keep the splinters from hitting his colleagues." He was voicing a general opinion that the actual details of the Norwegian campaign in itself were not important. What mattered was that after three years of Chamberlain's leadership, during which the country had been rearming itself with what it had been told was satisfying speed, results were still not adequate. In this larger issue, Churchill was certainly guiltless. Through the years of peace he had constantly warned both Parliament and the public. During the war, he had pressed various plans involving action which had been turned down by the French, or the General Staff, or his political colleagues.

Churchill himself wound up the debate on the government side, making over again with different detail the government's case. In the face of surprise, of air power, and of superb organization, the British had not been able to win. Some small advantages had been gained at sea, and there was still a foothold in the north which might be developed. Now was the moment to stand behind the government and not lose faith in times of trouble.

It was now eleven o'clock. Bells rang throughout the House to remind any members who had spared a thought for their lost dinners that the Commons were dividing. The dreadful moment had come in which sorely puzzled representatives must bethink themselves of their party or of the nation. The Opposition demanded a vote of no confidence. The Prime Minister had let it be known that if Conservatives who doubted would vote for him today, he would meet them tomorrow to discuss their recommendations. Was it wiser to pull the government down or try to amend it? Nor could it be forgotten that to vote against one's party might possibly mean political ruin.

Many refused to vote at all. Many chose the conventional side. Many crowded into the opposition lobby, risking careers for what they knew might be mistaken convictions. Bowing to the tellers, each made his way back to get a seat for the final announcement. Deliberately the tellers walked up between the rows with the government's Chief Whip on the right as a sign that the motion was defeated. But when beside the Speaker's chair the Chief Whip read the figures, there was a gasp. The government's majority was little more than a third of what it ought to have been. Considering the rigid nature of the British party system, such a victory was a resounding moral defeat. With justification the Labour Party raised a shout of "Resign, resign!" Chamberlain said nothing, but he must have known at once that his day was over. Silent, grim, and old, he got to his feet and walked from the House.

Considering this split in Conservative ranks, considering the need for unity in war, the vote of May 8th was a mortal blow. Nothing would now suffice but an all-party government in which the whole nation might feel fresh confidence. But Labour leaders were determined in their refusal to serve under Chamberlain.

On May 9th these issues were debated privately, while nothing was yet said and Parliament suffered from a sense of anticlimax. But on May 10th, something new and vitally important threatened to bury negotiations, leaving political problems unsettled. The western front was suddenly aflame. Hitler had invaded Holland and Belgium.

Chamberlain hesitated. The business of forming a new government involved the changing of over seventy officers of state, and the arrangements which would have to be made might take three weeks. Even then, many ministers would be new at their jobs. If any emergency were to arise, would it not be wiser to have an experienced government in possession? On the other hand, if prolonged and difficult fighting were now to take place, with the sort of heavy losses which the previous war had produced, was it not essential to have a government which commanded confidence? On the whole, Chamberlain still thought he ought to resign.

Then what should he do? When he went to the King to lay down the seals of office, the King would ask him who should be invited to form a government in his place. What should he say? There was Churchill. During the last few months, Chamberlain had come to entrust all sorts of things to Churchill. He liked him better and knew him better, too. But was Churchill sound? So many people, from Mr. Asquith down, had raised the question of whether one really could trust in Churchill's judgment. Mr. Chamberlain, less gifted than Asquith, less daring than Lloyd George, felt disinclined to take the risk. He knew, moreover, that Churchill never had been popular with Labour. His personal preference was Lord Halifax, an earnest, upright, intelligent peer with a distinguished record as Viceroy of India and Foreign Secretary, widely respected, though with no more talent for war than Chamberlain's own. Was it still possible for a peer to govern England in this day and age?

There was no time to be lost in roundabout inquiries. By eleven that morning, Chamberlain had summoned Churchill and Halifax both at once and put it to them that one or the other must be Prime Minister. Dead silence followed. Each sat waiting for the other to speak — Churchill short, massive, self-confident; Halifax long, lean, shy, and painfully conscious of duty. The anxious moment stretched out so long that it seemed as though nothing would be said. He who had no doubts of his powers could hardly begin. Halifax finally, with what regrets no man will ever know, declined the honor, very properly maintaining that he who led the country in war must sit in the Commons.

This settled the matter. Churchill said very little. By forty years of Parliament, by war, by great mistakes, by great achievements he had prepared himself for this hour. He put out his hand to grasp power with the feeling that having long known what ought to be done, he now at last had power to do it. That very evening, he was sent for by the King and officially entrusted with the task of forming a national government. That night he did not stay awake seeing visions of Death, though the cannons thundered in Belgium. He slept in profound relief, as though free of a burden.

The business of allotting offices went rapidly on while the first, indecisive news came trickling through from the western front. For a day or two at least the battle must develop, and in this breathing space there was much to be done. On May 13th, Churchill faced Parliament — a dubious Parliament, by no means content with what it had done. Mr. Chamberlain was loyally serving in Churchill's Cabinet, and the Conservatives followed his lead. Yet Chamberlain's supporters, still more than half of Parliament, were naturally angry that he had been forced out of office at such a time. All realized that what had broken out at last was the real war. Uneasy memories of the lost Norwegian campaign or the vast German drive of 1914 weighed heavily on them. Leaderless, anxious, uncertain, the House prepared to listen while its new Prime Minister asked for its formal vote of approval.

He spoke very briefly, for he could not have had much time. He gave them a matter-of-fact résumé of what he was doing and what he hoped to do in the practical business of getting a government set up with speed. What he said was neither disturbing nor reassuring; but people were willing to hasten through routine without demanding too much for the present. He would not, however, let them go in the mood in which they had come, though instinct told him that his message in this hurried moment must be blunt. He added slowly, "I would say to the House, as I have said to those who have joined this Government: 'I have nothing to offer but blood, toil, tears, and sweat.'"

There was a real silence for a second while members took in what none of their leaders in the past fifteen years could ever have said. Then there was a murmur, not a cheer, but perhaps the expression of a profound and welcome shock. He went on more sonorously to define his policy as waging war, his aim as victory, and to say to them, "Come then, let us go forward together with our united strength." But before he reached that final appeal, they were cheering him wildly.

ON THE fifteenth of May, when Churchill had been Prime Minister less than a week and was still living at the Admiralty flat, too busy to move into his official house, he was awakened by the announcement that the Prime Minister of France was on the telephone. He picked up the instrument by his bed. Mr. Reynaud, too distraught to break bad news gently, told him in English, "We have been defeated."

Defeat after five days seemed incredible. To be sure, the enemy might punch a hole in the line, as he had done in March, 1918. This would be a disaster, and yet after a few days when his armor halted for supplies, one could counterattack. The French army — and the British for the matter of that — was fresh and with its reserves intact. Things were not, could not be as desperate as 1918 when everyone was weary and resources were strained to the utmost. He tried to say as much to Reynaud, but all he got in return was, "We have been defeated. We have lost the battle."

This sounded like the old Antwerp days come again. He must go over and put heart into the French, leaving his government half reconstructed and trusting his new colleagues to handle what came up. He flew over on the seventeenth and found the situation worse than he could have imagined. He was taken to the French Foreign Office in the Quai d'Orsay and shown into a room with a view of the garden, in which bonfires of archives were already burning lest the Nazis capture them with Paris. One could see French civil servants with their little gray beards and their formal black suits wheeling out barrows of papers or trotting over with some special handful which they must put personally into the flame. Inside, General Gamelin, the tiny, wizened commander-in-chief, had set up an easel with a map of the western front on which, north of the Maginot Line but south of Belgium, was drawn a bulge.

Gamelin explained to the assembled statesmen. The Germans had concentrated overwhelming force at this point on the frontier, which was weakly defended because the terrain had been thought too rugged for armored troops. They had scattered the army which was to have held them there, poured their tanks through, and were fanning out at will in the countryside. Meanwhile, their dive bombers had thrown French communications into confusion. The Germans would either turn south for Paris or race west for the Channel ports, cutting off Belgium, the British Expeditionary Force, and the French northern armies.

There was one obvious thing to be done. The French and the British must counterattack from the north and the south to pinch off this bulge. The German armor, deprived of supplies, would then in its turn be in a dangerous position. Churchill turned to Gamelin and asked him in his horrible, but understandable French, "Where is your strategic reserve?"

Gamelin shrugged shoulders in despair. "There isn't any."

The new Prime Minister of Great Britain refrained from comment. Indeed, for once in his life he was speechless. This first close view of the incompetent leadership to which Britain's only army had been entrusted was one of his greatest shocks of the war. In the First World War, after millions of casualties and years of defeat, the two nations had been driven to recognize that they must have a unified command. This had quite naturally been French, since the French had the larger army and the war was being fought on their soil. In the Second World War, both nations had remembered their lesson. General Gort, the British commander, had been put under French orders. If he was treated a trifle condescendingly, and if the British were not told what French dispositions were, it had been largely their own fault for having only a tiny force by no means well equipped. It had occurred to no one that the pride of the French command was mere empty conceit, that they had actually stationed their army in a long, straggling line on their frontier without mobile reserves.

Churchill did what he could to encourage and to help, aware that Frenchmen were dying while many English troops who might have been aiding them were not ready. He had need of magnanimity, for in their agony the French were more ungenerous. The situation went from bad to worse so rapidly that by the twentieth the Germans had already reached the Channel coast. They had divided the Allied armies into two parts and were about to smash northward through the undefended Channel ports and surround the northern section. Three things now saved the British Expeditionary Force from extinction: the quality of its troops, the ability of its commanders, and the determination of Churchill and his advisers. The old Dunkirk Circus of 1914 had familiarized Churchill with the features of the countryside, and he was aware that the Gravelines waterline south of Dunkirk was a formidable obstacle. Much of it consisted of reclaimed land which could be flooded if a few days were given. Accordingly the British rushed over troops into Boulogne and Calais to hold up the German advance while the defenses of Dunkirk could be improvised. For two days the Guards held out in Boulogne against hopeless odds and were then evacuated by sea. But the time they had won was insufficient. Churchill had the courage to determine that Calais must be fought to the death and to send these orders to the troops, some thirty of whom alone were rescued.

Thus prompt decision and desperate measures saved Dunkirk. Meanwhile, though a timely conference was called to plan evacuation thence by sea, Churchill was determined to fight for France if it were possible. Indeed, he persisted until almost too late in demanding of General Gort an attack which the French were unable to co-ordinate or support. When it was decided to give up the hopeless attempt and race back to the sea, it looked very likely that only noncombatant troops near the base could ever be rescued. On Tuesday, May 28th, Churchill spoke to the House and briefly warned it to prepare itself for "hard and heavy tidings," by which he meant the total loss of England's army.

In these last two weeks of May, the British public had waked up at last to modern war. Their past experiences had prepared them for casualties, for slow starvation, even for bombing. They had never imagined that they might be conquered in a couple of weeks before they were properly fighting. This prospect aroused a fierce resentment. They were fortunate in having a leader who could not be blamed, who of all men was least at fault for the muddles of the thirties. Nor had Churchill become Prime Minister in time to make any decisions, right or wrong, before the catastrophe was on him. He had, however, in his government not merely Neville Chamberlain, but many other politicians who had supported appeasement. Numerous people who had not been any more far-seeing, but merely less prominent, were anxious to turn on the guilty. Churchill's generosity and good sense would have nothing to do with undermining the position of officers of state at such a time. He used all his influence to prevent what would have been a waste of national energy and destructive of the unity of the moment.

He himself was confident in his power to direct experienced people who had been listening to him for years with a shrug of the shoulders. He took for granted that all they needed in desperate times was leadership; and he proved right. In little more than a week his colleagues, including Chamberlain and Halifax, had drawn up a bill of a very different nature from any presented to Parliament so far in the war. The new government demanded extraordinary powers over life and property, over profits, wages, hours and conditions of labor. These were granted by Parliament almost without debate and in one afternoon. There was no question of those who had striven for peace hanging back from the war.

On the twenty-eighth, the very day in which he spoke to Parliament about the hard and heavy news expected from Dunkirk, Churchill called together about two dozen senior ministers of Cabinet rank who were not in the War Cabinet and with whom he had not so far been able to meet as a body. He explained to them exactly how the armies were situated in France and how little they could expect from a rescue operation, adding in an almost casual tone, "of course whatever happens at Dunkirk, we shall fight on." He admits himself surprised by what took place. Middle-aged people, staid senior politicians jumped out of their chairs and rushed toward him, trying to shake his hand or pat him on the back. It is so easy for a man to utter brave words and yet in secret prepare the ground for giving in when things grow desperate. The leaders of the people, no matter what their past record, were looking for an example of firmness even to the death; and they had found it.

Thus the British government, which might have been split into quarreling fragments, was confirmed in unity by the strength of Churchill. Happily the nation was saved by a brilliant feat from the worst consequences of earlier follies. The evacuation of the British army from Dunkirk, in spite of all the Germans could do, resulted in the saving of five-sixths of the whole, including its irreplaceable professional men, among them most of the generals who were to lead Britain to victory five years later. Their rescue was felt to be a second chance, as indeed it was. British pride in a notable achievement reflected glory on the new government in spite of defeat. The people's confidence in themselves and their new leader was confirmed — and what was equally important, individuals who wanted to serve in some special way began to feel needed. In the Dunkirk operation, yachts, fishing smacks, lifeboats, and every make-shift vessel which could boast an auxiliary engine had set out to the rescue, manned very often by nonprofessional crews; and all had been welcome. Meanwhile Churchill, appalled by the lack of resistance put up in France, was pushing forward the formation of a Home Guard to deal with invasion. Aircraft production was recognized as the great need of the hour, and workers were encouraged to make special efforts. All such activities were desperately satisfying to people caught in a surge of emotion. Church-ill instinctively recognized the need to give expression to the national resolve without delay.

How far he formed England's resolve and how far merely reproduced it in magnificent, memorable words could not be decided. He said himself later that the British lion was angry and that it had fallen to his lot to utter the roar. This was true, and yet he did more than express the mood of the moment. He confirmed it. He proclaimed to the people: "We shall go on to the end, we shall fight in France, we shall fight on the seas and oceans, we shall fight with growing confidence and strength in the air, we shall defend our Island, whatever the cost may be, we shall fight on the beaches, we shall fight on the landing grounds, we shall fight in the fields and in the streets, we shall fight in the

hills; we shall never surrender . . ." [1] Englishmen may not
have felt that his resolution differed from their own; but
they certainly were strengthened by hearing their thoughts
expressed with grandeur. Churchill did more than this.
He lifted their struggle onto a higher plane by telling his
people that they fought for more than survival. The
Christian civilization of the Western World was under
threat of destruction. "We have become sole champions
now in arms to defend the world cause. We shall do our
best to be worthy of this high honor." He himself had
never forgotten the great traditions of his ancestry and race.
Speaking therefore as he felt, Marlborough's descendant
reminded his fellow countrymen that theirs was but an
episode in a history which had been noble. He appealed
to them, "Let us therefore brace ourselves to our duties and
so bear ourselves that, if the British Empire and its Commonwealth last for a thousand years, men still will say,
'This was their finest hour.'"

It was the moment for the grand style. Churchill's elaborate manner of speech had appeared out of place a few
years back. Now suddenly it came into its own, and he
came with it. The man who never had a party won for
himself almost overnight the undying love of a nation.
Nor was this all. He very nearly convinced most neutral
observers of Britain's intentions. France after six weeks of
war had totally succumbed, had collapsed more utterly
than even Poland, Norway, Holland, or Belgium. The reve-
lation that France was hollow had been a shock to world

[1] *Their Finest Hour.* Boston: Houghton Mifflin Co., 1949.

opinion, particularly in the United States. American leaders, who foresaw that Nazi Germany as a world power
would be their enemy, had now to face a decision about
whether Great Britain was sound. Hers was indeed a world
cause; and her need was terrible, since most of her army
equipment had been abandoned in France. Yet if she had
intended to put up no more than a token fight, it would
have been wiser to keep American arms for America's need.
As it was, a half-million rifles and nine hundred guns
from World War I were taken from storage and dispatched
to Britain without delay. Had it not been for the leadership
of Churchill, it seems unlikely that this gamble could have
been made.

The collapse of France brought an ominous pause in the
war. Hitler had made no preparations for subduing Britain
as yet, and he hoped she would soon admit her cause was
lost. The British, desperately toiling to make ready their
air force and rearm their men, had a breathing space of a
sort. Emergencies no longer arose from day to day; and
it became more possible for those who governed with
Churchill to form an estimate of his capacity. This clearly
was outstanding and peculiar. Churchill was a great
administrator and chooser of men. The organization of his
government worked well, far better than Asquith's and
better than Lloyd George's. The clash of opinion between
the politicians as such and the army planners which had
nearly lost the First World War did not arise. However,
though Churchill well understood how to divide and delegate, he reserved an unbounded right to interfere. He
goaded his ministers quite deliberately, either to keep them

on the alert or to prevent them from ignoring some aspect of their work. His energy was enormous, his interests varied, and he never restrained himself from pursuing them. Nothing was too small for a note or an inquiry: unfair proceedings of a navy selection board, a dingy Admiralty flag, consideration of the beauty of the countryside, or the rationing of candy. Yet trivial matters merely served as an outlet for excess energy. They never obscured the main issue, which was for him and always remained the winning of the war.

This fundamental purpose of winning was already with him in the dark days of June and July when Britain, almost defenseless, faced a continent in arms across twenty miles of narrow strait. He was realistic enough to have his chiefs of staff draw up a cold-blooded appraisal of England's chances, ending with the comment that Germany held most of the cards, but that much could depend on fighting spirit. He did not seek to blind himself to military facts; yet to him warfare meant hitting the enemy hard and first. It was never defensive. Such an attitude at such a time required great courage. Churchill insisted on reinforcing the tiny army in Egypt which was facing five times its own number deployed from Italian bases on the North African shore. Tanks were sent out, first fruits of British factories, though these were desperately needed in the struggle for survival, should Hitler invade. Meanwhile, Count Ciano, the Italian Foreign Minister, ruefully noted that the captains of the British fleet were not less aggressive and ruthless than their ancestors of old. He might have added that the directions given to them were no less daring.

Britain struck back where and as she could, while piling up weapons at a rate which would once have seemed miraculous, but now was all too slow. Yet woe betide anybody who, obsessed by present need, described experiment as a waste of money or time. The ingenuity which led Churchill once to father the tank now bade him direct his attention to novel ideas of every sort, from a "sticky" bomb for use against tanks by guerrillas to the vast artificial harbors which were built to supply the invasion of France at his suggestion. Trials of new weapons fascinated him in themselves, and some of his advisers undoubtedly felt now and then that he backed wild ideas. Churchill for his part had learned to suspect the military mind in the First World War. He made it his business to see that every notion, no matter how farfetched, at least had a hearing.

Britain's respite lasted only for a few weeks; yet these were just long enough for her preparations. The Battle of Britain in which the German air force tried to annihilate the British was Hitler's first defeat. It decided the question of a German invasion of Britain, which was put off until the following year — in fact, forever. Denied the mastery of the skies by day, the Germans concentrated on bombing by night as winter drew on. For more than sixty continuous nights London was bombed at a time when air-raid shelters and methods of defense could scarcely be said to exist. Thereafter attacks broadened out through the country, hardly a town of any considerable size escaping damage. During these dark days, the people saw much of their Prime Minister. With his usual common sense about working conditions, he had fitted himself up a train so as to have an office from which he could still be in touch while traveling about. Using this, or curling up in the back seat of his car for a nap, which his short stature made possible, he visited here and there after horrible nights and spoke to everyone. Humble but fervent admirers of his great courage and strength now came in contact with his rich and glorious eccentricity. Their admiration was not in any way decreased by amusement; rather the bond of love was strengthened. It was refreshing to find that the great man was sometimes absurd.

It was about this time that Winston, always slightly eccentric in dress, turned his spare attention to the question of practical clothes and had designed for him a zip-up boiler suit and zippered shoes. These garments, as he blithely advertised, saved several seconds over putting on coat and pants or tying laces. Recommending them to all in happy disregard of clothes rationing, he had a set made up for himself, encouraging a more cheerful note in masculine dress by choosing powder-blue. Not too surprisingly, his staid compatriots totally failed to follow his example. Indeed, the tubby figure of Winston was of all shapes the least suited to display a boiler suit in powder-blue. He chose to wear with it a black soft hat and of course a cigar, presenting an appearance which even people who knew him well never quite got used to.

It was the unselfconsciousness that everyone liked. Tears came to his eyes at scenes of destruction; and he was not, like other Englishmen, ashamed of these. His trotting gait; his sudden snatches of humming; his harsh, peculiar voice with the lisp; his drawling pronunciation of common enemy

names all gave pleasure. His boundless energy, his inquisi-
tive desire to see for himself, his devastating humor made
him unique. The word filtered through that he was impervious to any sense of danger, could not be prevented
from going up on the roof to watch air raids, and eventually
had to have a gallery built there to protect him from
splinters.

Fact and legend very soon became happily mingled. The
people cared about him personally, not just as a leader;
and they were confident of his affection for them. It was
at this time that Churchill realized the plight of the little
man whose shop and livelihood was wiped out by a bomb.
Over the horrified protests of the Treasury, he insisted that
a form of insurance be worked out in such a way that the
loss of one must be made good by all. This was done, and
by a fortunate turn in the war, it did not bring the bank-
ruptcy which the officials had threatened. But the general
principle by which Winston had been guided was not pru-
dence, but an understanding of what was really meant by
a people's war.

While thus in what amounts to spare time he was cement-
ing a bond between the people and himself, Churchill ran
a World War. His methods of doing so may best be illustrated by a British victory that winter and a defeat in spring.
In Egypt that November, Generals Wavell and O'Connor,
backed by the precious tanks which Winston had spared
from England's crisis, fell on the Italians and with two
divisions destroyed ten, advancing five hundred miles and
taking a hundred and thirty thousand prisoners for the
loss of less than two thousand. Scarcely had they done so

than Churchill denuded them of troops in order to go to the assistance of Greece, attacked by Italy. But the Germans, bursting down through the Balkan countries, not only expelled the British from Greece with ease, but also shipped an armored force to North Africa and very shortly won back the ground which the British were not now strong enough to hold on to.

Both incidents are typical of Churchill, who always tried to attack and hated waiting. No sooner was a force equipped with tanks and guns than he wanted them used without waiting for spare parts and reserves. The high proportion of troops occupied in the desert campaigns with repair or supply never ceased to annoy him. Nor could he restrain himself until one operation was fully complete before pressing another. On the other hand, in many ways his methods were effective. He never lost sight of the fact that the enemy has his troubles too, and he also exaggerates your strength while he wonders where the blow will fall. On this occasion, though the British lost in prestige by their defeat in Greece and threw away their chances in North Africa, they did in fact accomplish something important. They succeeded in disarranging Hitler's scheme for attacking Russia. In the summer of 1941, Russia lost so much ground to the Germans that she very nearly had to accept defeat. The winter saved her; and the few weeks that Churchill had won played their part. The fact that he could not have foreseen this makes no difference to the truth of his general creed that it pays to attack.

Notwithstanding, soldiers condemn the campaign in Greece from a military point of view, and they are right.

But Winston was primarily the political head of the war. The British had a treaty with Greece, as they had had with Poland. They could not allow it to be said that every small nation which tried to join their side would be used and abandoned. Thus the Greek campaign is an instance of the fashion in which the political view may quarrel with the strategic. This was the conflict which every democracy at war fought out, and which Churchill solved.

He was able to solve it because his personal power was enormous. He had behind him a unanimous Parliament, which none of his predecessors in war had ever possessed. And behind the Parliament, he had as far as is possible a unanimous people. He was therefore able to assume powers which were almost those of a dictator. As head of the Cabinet he had the direction of policy. In so far as this concerned the course of the war, he worked with a War Cabinet, an inner circle of five or seven people who considered the strategy of the whole war at the top level. But independent of this was the Chiefs of Staff Committee, consisting of the Chief of the Imperial General Staff, the First Sea Lord, and the Chief of the Air Staff, who were respectively the Service heads of Britain's armed forces. These worked directly with the Prime Minister in his capacity of Minister of Defence. They also had access through their chairman to the War Cabinet, where they could explain the professional point of view. Fundamentally, however, it was the Prime Minister with whom both Committee and Cabinet dealt. It was part of his function to defend the views of the one in the meetings of the other. What is more, the final decision and responsibility lay on his shoulders.

This arrangement worked well, though not without friction. It would have been easier for the Chiefs of Staff if their Prime Minister had less decided views. But like his rival, Hitler, also an amateur, Churchill was unable to leave the military to manage alone. His ideas on strategy, like Hitler's, varied from the brilliant to the mad. Fundadamentally, his trouble was that in the first place he had too many ideas, and in the second the latest notion was for the time all-important. Having decided on an operation in the Egyptian Desert, the preparation for which would swallow up for months all available transport, tanks, and aircraft, he was capable of pressing on his chiefs a raid on Norway, the seizure of a base in French Madagascar, and the shipping of increased supplies to Russia. Meanwhile, unable to wait for the build-up in Egypt, he would take to worrying his commanders on the spot by telegraphing in the hope they would attack before they were ready.

It was only natural that his chiefs of staff and he should very frequently be locked in battle. On such occasions, Churchill's tempestuous nature sent him charging into the fray with every weapon. He would argue brilliantly, persuasively till three in the morning with exhausted men who had been at their desks at nine and whose routine did not leave leisure for afternoon naps. He would bombard them with unfair questions which could not be answered by plain yes or no. He would take refuge in the argument that the military mind had no imagination, or he would even occasionally suggest their motives were not pure. When all the battery of his other weapons had been expended, he would lose his temper, slam papers together, and walk out. But next morning without another word he supported their view.

In fact, the difference between Churchill and Hitler as military men consisted in this, that Churchill surrounded himself with the ablest advisers he could find — and would not act without their advice. If he could wear them down, he would. If not, unless there were some political factor to be considered, he acted with them. Small wonder that his chiefs of staff found him difficult to work with and yet were devoted to him; found him an outrageous amateur and yet were kept on their toes by his flights of fancy.

Even Churchill's day wore out his friends and colleagues. He started it almost as early as they, but spent his mornings comfortably propped up in bed, gorgeous in scarlet dressing gown, complete with cigar, and strewn with papers, dictating, absorbing reports, telephoning, throwing out queries to which he wanted the answer at once, or summoning people to his bedside like a monarch giving audience. Having thus got through an immense amount of business with the least possible fatigue to himself, he dressed for a Cabinet meeting, a lunch with the King, or whatever his first engagement might be, not without being hurried by his anxious valet, who knew he was frequently late. There followed an exhausting day of conferences or inspections, varied by stopping to try out a weapon for himself or poking an interested nose into something he happened to think of. Before dinner, he went back to bed for a nap, or if he was traveling, put a piece of black velvet over his eyes and fell asleep. Waking refreshed and full of ideas, he started out on a second day lasting from dinner till at least two in the morning. These were the times for long discussions with individuals or groups in which he aired his own theories, while acquiring through some peculiar process a detailed knowledge of his companions' work. People subjected to these appalling hours later on found wry satisfaction in watching American military men or political leaders trying to look polite while sitting up with Churchill on top of a long day of other business.

As for Churchill himself, he seemed to take no notice of the strain involved by being whirled round in his orbit. Yet now and then it would occur to him that someone must be tired or was looking worn. Curiously, people who had been exhausted by his company countless times were very much touched by the warmth of his occasional kindness. They recognized it as a glimpse of the nature of a man who was really too busy to indulge in thoughtfulness. They were overcome because they felt it amazing that he who bore such a responsibility, on whom every disaster must sit like a literal weight, should consider individuals even for a moment.

Thus through frantic work, impossible hours, fierce arguments, and mutual respect, the direction of the war became effective. Democracy, which had been despised by Hitler, proved efficient because Churchill, though granted enormous powers, refused to employ them. Unless Parliament, the Cabinet, the Chiefs of Staff were behind him, he would not impose his ideas, though he could have done so.

Britain, not Germany, enjoyed a combination of the inspiring, guiding single mind, the general view, and the specialist knowledge. Of all the gifts of Churchill, not the least remarkable is this restraint. In the last resort, it is the final answer to those repeated doubts about his judgment. To be sure, his enthusiasms might be wild, but his decisions were sound. It may be said in fact of Churchill that he did not value his power for its own sake or his ideas for theirs, but put both at the service of his country. Under his government, Great Britain held out alone against impossible odds for a year. She held out six months longer while the German attack on Russia came within an ace of outright conquest. When Japan entered the war and upset the balance of power in the Pacific at Pearl Harbor, Britain somehow weathered that mortal storm on top of all else. No national government which had not been both brave and brilliant could have achieved this.

In WAR, it is foreign policy which looks to the future. There is little constructive to be done at home beyond organizing the nation to win. The creation of a network of alliances, the establishment of agreed principles, the architecture of a just peace are the tasks which challenge a statesman. Plunged though he immediately was into the chaos of the French collapse, Churchill never lost this long view. Temperamentally he was no more inclined to leave matters of such moment to his Foreign Secretary than Chamberlain had been. He, too, believed in personal contact at the highest level. It is typical of him that within less than a week of taking office, he found the time to draft a personal letter to Mussolini, appealing to him not to enter the war on the German side. Churchill had met the Italian dictator in 1927, and on the whole through the troubles of the thirties he had held pro-Italian views. These were slender foundations on which to build in 1940 after Mussolini had made up his mind that Hitler would win. Churchill must have expected this letter to have no effect; but since he had nothing to lose by making the contact, he found time for it in those crowded, desperate days when each second counted. For in diplomacy as Churchill understood it, nothing must ever be left untried. Untiring persistence was the secret of his method.

By far the most fruitful result of Churchill's intervention in foreign affairs was his establishment of personal intimacy with Franklin Roosevelt. Seldom has a friendship between rulers done more to bring two countries together at a vital moment. To be sure, the interests of the great democracies coincided; but their ignorance of each other was still profound, their organizations in no way dovetailed. Even their alliance in the previous World War had merely led to disagreements over the peace which were still rankling. Thus the first immediate reaction of the United States in 1939 was to keep out of war, even though it was realized that Britain and France must and should stand up to Hitler. The American Neutrality Act forbidding the sale of munitions to either side was shortly seen to discriminate against England, who had command of the sea and was in sole position to trade. It was therefore emended on a cash-and-carry principle which was intended to eliminate all risk, while permitting the Allies to draw on American resources. Having thus done all that appeared to be called for, the American people began to press for results. They wanted the democracies to go in and win; they had a resentful suspicion that a deal was being fixed up, as it had been at Munich. There was known to be a peace party in France; Chamberlain the appeaser was still Prime Minister of England; the war was not going to be pressed.

American doubts gave international importance to Churchill, the very last person who would tolerate an agreed peace without serious fighting. Accordingly, in the first days of the war, President Roosevelt wrote Churchill a letter, taking occasion to congratulate him on returning to

the Admiralty, mentioning his own similar service as Assist-
ant Secretary of the Navy in 1917, and inviting correspondence. Nothing could have suited Churchill better. He was
well aware of the priceless importance of such a contact, both
to his own position and to his country. Besides, he enjoyed writing letters. His exuberant personality overflowed
into words; and though he was the soul of discretion where
war secrets must be kept, he was always eager to express
views. He liked to bombard his friends with written
memoranda, and it was never his habit to refrain from
doing so when an idea struck him. On the contrary, he
would fetch his secretary out of bed because a notion for a
letter, not necessarily urgent, popped into his head. He had
no intention of being inconsiderate, but just could not
settle to anything else with a letter on his mind.

At this time, then, in 1939, a famous correspondence
was born. Churchill for security reasons signed his letters
"Naval Person." On leaving the Admiralty to become Prime
Minister, he emended this signature to "Former Naval
Person," which it remained. In the period of nearly five
years between May, 1940, and Roosevelt's death, Former
Naval Person's letters if spaced out evenly would have
easily numbered three weekly, sometimes four. Roosevelt's
answers are not quite as many. Nor was this an official
correspondence in the formal sense of the word. That is,
there was no arrangement that Churchill should show his
colleagues what he had written before he sent it off. To be
sure, a great many letters were composed after Cabinet
discussions in which the Prime Minister was asked to
express to Roosevelt the official view. Others were sub-

mitted as a matter of course to the Chiefs of Staff, the Foreign Office, or some other department whose opinions on the matter in hand were relevant. Numbers were circulated immediately after dispatch. Nothing alters the fact, however, that the head of the British government could say what he pleased to the President. The only check on Churchill was his own sense of how far he ought to speak for his colleagues. It is a real tribute to this naturally combative, impulsive, even arbitrary man that the chief difficulty which seems to have arisen is that sometimes Churchill was pressed to take matters up which he thought too trivial to put to the President.

The collapse of France in 1940 placed President Roosevelt in a difficult position. It was no longer possible for America to bring about a victory for the Allies by keeping out of Europe and selling them munitions for cash. Nor was it possible to allow the British Navy to fall into Hitler's hands, together with the French and the Italian — especially at a moment when relations with Japan were definitely strained. Yet American feeling was dead against being involved, and 1940 was an election year. Besides, the spectacular collapse of France affected onlookers as though they had strayed into quicksand. Whatever men's suspicions of France, they had not dreamed of this. Was anything solid? How dared one put any faith in Britain's intentions?

In such a crisis, the half-American Churchill understood the difficulties of the President, while M. Reynaud and the French Cabinet did not. Reynaud appealed to Roosevelt and was dashed by an answer in which Churchill felt the President had committed himself as far as he could. Seeing clearly and at very short range America's interest in the struggle, the French were simply impatient with the slow process of American thought. In their need, they had reason to be so; but in the year which followed when England stood alone, Churchill too had reason. Over and over again while the future of England hung in the balance, it would have been natural for him to blame America or the President for hanging back. He never did so, but always held clearly before himself the American view. Though the interests of the two countries were in a very broad sense identical, it did not follow that their thoughts ran along the same channels and at the same time. And though the governments of both were democracies and shared a common tradition, their constitutions and their outlooks differed widely. To see this is easy; but very few statesmen at such a time could have kept it always in mind.

Churchill's policy toward the United States from the first was bold and simple. It was necessary to convince the neutral world that Britain's defiance of Hitler did not mean a token resistance in order to gain better terms. The American gesture of faith which released from storage half a million rifles, eighty thousand machine guns, nine hundred field guns, and their ammunition to re-equip the British army after Dunkirk could not have been made had there been serious question of these weapons simply falling by treaty to Hitler. Churchill, however, was well aware that he must convince America not merely that Britain was resolved, but that she could win. He must also take the initiative in pressing for American aid, yet without offending his well-wishers by grasping at too much. He must concentrate from the first on what was essential.

Accordingly, in that first fruitful week of his government, Churchill put to the President a request for the loan of fifty American destroyers to bridge the gap until new British construction should be ready. The President answered that an act of Congress would be required and that the moment was not opportune. Notwithstanding, Churchill brought the matter up again not three weeks later, pointing out that the appearance of Italy in the war meant a hundred more submarines to cope with. This extra pressure might well make England unable to deal with Hitler's invasion. Once more nothing could be devised, but the subject was taken up in Washington by the British Ambassador. As the weeks wore on into July, American opinion was becoming more concerned about the British fleet. Without some help in destroyers, all might be lost. Yet if help were given, all might still be lost, and the destroyers in addition. It seemed impossible that Congress could be induced to gamble with the United States Navy.

By the end of July, the German occupation of submarine bases in Norway and France was beginning to be felt. Eleven destroyers were sunk in the course of ten days. Churchill called the figure to Roosevelt's attention. Something clearly must be done. The suggestion was made in Washington that Britain should offer bases in the West Indies, Newfoundland, and elsewhere in outright exchange for fifty American destroyers. Since America manifestly had the best of this bargain, Congress could scarcely object for security reasons. Great Britain for her part could gain the destroyers and must benefit in every way from American bases out in the Atlantic. To be sure, this transaction was an openly unneutral act, but it served to make obvious Hitler's reluctance to challenge the United States. Thus, having taken one step without being called to account, America was ready to consider another move in the same direction.

The cash-and-carry arrangement established for the sale of munitions was satisfactory only to a certain extent from the British view. Germany, of course, was cut off from American trade by the British command of the seas. So far so good; but British dollar credits, though vast, were not inexhaustible. The Chamberlain government was haunted by the fear of their running out. It placed its orders with economy and care. Churchill reversed this policy immediately, instructing his ministers to order what they needed and worry later about how to make payment. This bold decision was perfectly sound. Wars cannot be waged by economy. Besides, the more England ordered, the faster the wheels of American industry would turn. The more deeply America committed herself to armaments production, the more impossible it would be to shut this suddenly off. In fact, the American position of 1939 was based on a misunderstanding of war which Churchill immediately perceived and showed courage in exploiting.

The crisis was not long in coming. Less than six months after Churchill came into power, British dollar credits were already inadequate to pay for what had been ordered. In an important letter of early December, 1940, Churchill pointed this out to the President. By now America had gone too far to turn in her tracks, nor was it advisable that she should do so. Roosevelt's answer to the problem was "Lend or Lease." The Secretary of War is able at discretion to lease army property for five years when it is not needed. By a liberal extension of this power, America was henceforward to "Lend or Lease" munitions to England without asking money. Matters had reached a point where the President could openly speak of the British as fighting America's war and refer to his proposal in terms of lending his neighbor a hose to put out a fire. Once more it was noticeable that Hitler was not prepared to go to war with the United States. Thus every milestone in Anglo-American relations, once safely past, made progress to the next one more enticing. The Lend-Lease Act was signed in March, 1941, and almost at the same moment the United States Fleet began to stretch out from its new bases and extend its security zone across the Atlantic with the assistance of bases still farther forward in Greenland and Iceland.

Hitler did nothing because his course was already determined and his forces preoccupied. He had taken the decision to turn his main effort against Russia. In the spring of 1941, he was busy establishing the safety of his flank by fastening his grip on the Balkans. The unexpected resistance of Yugoslavia and Greece with the aid of Britain disarranged the Nazi timetable somewhat; and it was not finally till June 22, 1941, that the German torrent poured over the Russian border without warning.

The German attack on Russia transformed the character of the war, though by no means at first to Britain's advan-

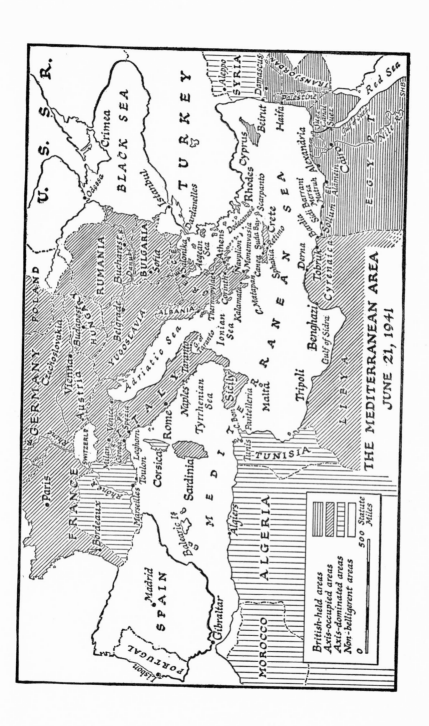

THE MEDITERRANEAN AREA
JUNE 21, 1941

British-held areas
Axis-occupied areas
Axis-dominated areas
Non-belligerent areas

0   500 Statute
              Miles

tage. To be sure, for the first time the German armies, swollen to a vast size by drafts from satellite populations, were opposed by an even greater numerical strength. On the immense plains of Russia there was room for these forces to deploy, so that such a contest was bound to be titanic. The effect of Germany's effort was felt in England, where the Blitz died away; in the Mediterranean; in Africa, where the supplies to German forces were reduced in the ensuing months to a trickle. But in Russia, Hitler's armies rolled irresistibly forward in a series of shattering victories which only the still-far-distant winter was to check on the threshold of Moscow.

Outlawed by the Western World since 1918, the Russian leaders felt none of the sentimental ties which bound, for instance, Britain and France. In the great world crisis brought on by Hitler, Russian policy had been coldly opportunistic. Not daring to trust the democracies after Munich, the Russians had turned their attention to strengthening their own border. Thus they had made a deal with Hitler for the partition of Poland, which in fact brought on the war. And during 1940 while Germany conquered the West, the Russians were selfishly increasing their armies, liquidating prominent Poles and anti-Russian leaders of the luckless little Baltic states, and picking a quarrel with Finland in order to gain ground in front of Leningrad. Naturally enough, by 1941 the British government viewed Russia with the deepest distrust. If it were possible for Stalin to get decent terms by surrender to Hitler, nobody imagined that loyalty to his ally would stand in his way. As 1941 moved into fall and the Russian losses mounted to two million, it began to seem likely that Stalin would be glad of peace on any terms.

It was under difficulties such as these that Churchill steadily and persistently undertook the task of building a personal relationship with Stalin. It was not easy. Of all British politicians Churchill's record in the last twenty years was most strongly anti-Russian. As Minister of War in 1919, he had striven his hardest to get the Allies to put down the Bolshevists by force before they fastened their grip on Russia. Failing to do so, he had watched with horror the extermination of millions of peasants as part of Stalin's program for changing the whole face of Russian economy. It was inevitable that he should look on Stalin as a man with more blood on his hands than any man living, with the possible exception of Hitler and a couple of his henchmen. Nevertheless, he applied himself to his task with his usual vigor, merely remarking that if the Devil himself were to lend aid against Hitler, he would go so far in return as to make a favorable reference to His Infernal Majesty in Parliament.

The first two weeks of the Russian campaign passed in silence, each national leader presumably adjusting his feelings somewhat toward his ally. Presently Churchill made the first move, referring tactfully to the magnificent courage of the Russians, which roused from then onward increasing admiration in his heart. The answer was courteous, in a very distant fashion almost apologetic for the past. It went on, however, to suggest immediate invasion of the Dutch, French, or Norwegian coast and the establishment at once of a second front. Thus at the outset of the long correspondence, the focus of misunderstanding was established. Neither Stalin nor his advisers knew or cared to learn about naval operations. They simply assumed that a landing in face of land-based planes on a hostile shore could be sustained if England were prepared to make the effort. They knew she had the ships. All the intricate problems of maintaining the German blockade, of ocean trade, of protecting far-flung ports, or of submarine warfare could not in the Russian view be counted as fighting. They looked upon England as holding back while Russia fought, and on their attitude facts and figures of every kind made little impression. Thus from the very first the correspondence of the two war leaders took a form which makes curious reading. Stalin, always demanding help, is always indignant at the amount he gets. Churchill meanwhile, like a dog with a bone for master, writes to inform him of two submarines which are sunk, or a raid on the Ruhr, of the passage of a convoy through to Malta, in fact of small-scale successes which must have seemed ludicrous to Stalin with his vast operations. Yet Churchill is probably right in regarding such achievements as something to put forward, better than nothing at all. Every so often he even elicits a sentence of praise from his grim correspondent.

Meanwhile, Churchill recognized that Russia needed aid, if not in terms of a second front, at least in munitions of war. The industrialized portions of Russia were still very largely in the west, where much was overrun and more in danger. There was serious question of how long the Russian troops could be supplied. The Russians provided long lists of vital needs which Britain and the United States now undertook to supply. It is worth noting that both portions were in effect subtracted from the British war effort, since in the beginning America merely diverted what had been promised to England, having nothing else which she could offer. Churchill naturally was aware of this fact and showed his usual courage in resisting the objections of his chiefs of staff, which as the war went on grew more pronounced. They pointed out that the Russians had refused to give the figures on which their calculation of their needs was based. The tanks and planes sent over were strange to Russian mechanics and were bound to be deficient in spare parts. In fact, it was questionable whether Britain's enormous sacrifice in the Russian cause was of comparable value to them. In addition, there was the terrible task of getting goods into Russia.

Communications with Russia were open by north and by south. A rickety, single-track railroad ran up from the Persian Gulf. Not only was it unsuited for heavy traffic, but its communications with the Russian railway system were poor. Furthermore, supplies to the Persian Gulf must go round Africa, which would be too slow and would tie up too much shipping. There remained the far northern ports of Archangel and Murmansk, the latter luckily ice-free all through the winter. These were nearer, but involved a difficult voyage up the whole length of the German-held Norwegian coast, exposed to submarines, to land-based planes, to powerful raiders, and to some of the worst weather in the world. At certain seasons perpetual day stripped the convoys of all cover, while the encroachments of the Polar icecap forced them to run in close to the land.

To the horrors of the passage was added enormous waste in ships and men and in the munitions which England had sacrificed in her own need. Notwithstanding, Churchill persisted, never losing sight of the vital fact that England's relation to Russia might win or lose the war for both of them.

Meanwhile, Stalin's correspondence assumed a bullying tone. European diplomacy of the old school to which Churchill belonged worked on the assumption that more is gained by patient politeness than by shouting. Manifestly the Russian held the contrary view. Thus the two correspondents circled each other like wrestlers seeking a hold, each fighting in his own style. Churchill, generous with facts and figures, persistent, profuse, lavish of compliments to the Russian army, ceaselessly maneuvered to break through Stalin's grudging reserve or downright rudeness. Every so often he would either by silence or very formal reproof let his opponent know that he had gone too far. Both would draw back slightly, aware that their relations were dominated by facts beyond their control. Russia contained German armies on a scale which England could not match; but the British navy and America's war production were vital to Russia's survival. Thus limited, the two found time to learn each other's game, discover points in common, and cautiously consider the future in the light of better acquaintance.

While Churchill thus sparred with Stalin, British relationships with the United States did not stand still. America was arming herself, and the time of her entry into the struggle was drawing nearer. Moreover, the war, which had so far spared the Pacific, loomed ominously there. The Japanese nation, long at odds with the Western World over its war with China, now beheld itself face to face with opportunity. French Indochina and the Dutch East Indies both belonged to countries conquered by Hitler and were in a real sense detached from their owners and going begging. And what of Malaya and Burma, of Hong Kong, Singapore, Australia, India? Great Britain, fighting for life against submarine warfare, besieged in her island, deeply engaged in North Africa, denuding herself to supply the Russians, and committed to garrisons throughout the Middle East could not be strong everywhere. So dangerous was the situation in the Pacific that many in Britain, backed up by military observers from the United States, now urged the sacrifice of British hard-won positions in North Africa and the Middle East in order to strengthen the Far East. Churchill would have none of it. The Middle East and aid to Russia were vital. Little could be done for the Far East save trust the American Navy and hope that it would intervene. In July, 1941, the Japanese moved into French Indochina and stood poised for an attack on the East Indies or Malaya. America at once imposed an embargo on Japan, while the British and the Dutch, though trembling for their position, followed her lead. Cut off in this fashion from rubber and oil, the Japanese were bound either to back down or to advance on Dutch and British possessions. The agonizing question was how far the United States would then feel committed to war.

Problems such as these, the allocation of the new supplies to Russia, British-American staff talks, and the increasingly active American role in the Atlantic all posed questions which pointed to the need of formal conference. President Roosevelt had sent over Harry Hopkins as his personal emissary, and during the many discussions held between him and Churchill it was agreed that the time was ripe for a meeting between the two leaders. The unity of Great Britain and America must now be proclaimed to the world. Let Germany tremble! And let Japan beware!

Details were soon arranged. Churchill on Britain's newest battleship, the *Prince of Wales,* set out across the Atlantic in a holiday spirit. Since he must travel under radio silence and could send no messages, he was relieved perforce of the day-to-day guidance of affairs. He had much to think about and drew up some memoranda. But he also found leisure for puttering about this fine new ship, as in the good old Admiralty days of 1912 when his enthusiasms had bored Mr. Asquith. He had brought his favorite movie on Lord Nelson, which he had seen several times, but which was still good for an hour or so of relaxation. For the first time perhaps in two years he read a novel. Meanwhile President Roosevelt, transshipping secretly from his yacht to the *Augusta,* was also on his way to the rendezvous in a bay of Newfoundland.

This meeting of the two leaders, which took place in August, 1941, was in itself historical and marked a more intimate stage in their personal relations. They came prepared to like each other, each believing that he was meeting a great man. But Churchill owed Roosevelt a deference that he was careful to pay, never forgetting that he, the mere minister of the Crown, was in conference with the head of a State. This formal tribute was Roosevelt's right, yet he was not impervious to the flattery of being so treated by the free world's hero. No doubt also, Churchill's old-fashioned ceremoniousness was in itself a little unusual. It had been acquired as minister of state in a monarchy over three decades ago — in the distant ages before the First World War unsettled men's manners. At all events, the exchange of compliments became increasingly friendly. On Sunday morning the President came over to the *Prince of Wales* attended by his staff and several hundred of all ranks. The Stars and Stripes were draped with the Union Jack on the pulpit, Churchill himself chose the hymns, while American and British chaplains shared in the reading.

The conference took four days and was almost continuous on several levels at once, each party having brought with it experts on military affairs and on supply. Thus all the practical problems of importance were taken up in groups of varying sizes. Meanwhile, the leaders were finding their general agreement on the objects of the war complete. They had also in common that priceless gift of politicians, personal charm. Both of them, as the accompanying experts ruefully noted, were men of ideas. British military men in particular, who had often spent laborious hours in toning down their leader's wilder notions, were by no means pleased at the way he and Roosevelt encouraged each other. They found their own American counterparts inexperienced in war and thought them too ready to swallow the impractical suggestions of politicians whole. Luckily, however, discussions went smoothly enough on the practical points, while the principals concentrated on a broad declaration which should set the tone of policy for the future.

The Atlantic Charter, as it came to be called, was Roosevelt's suggestion, but largely of Churchill's drawing up. It represented the most carefully considered statement of war aims so far reached. Having regard to the obscurity of the current situation, it was expressed in general terms. The two democracies declared themselves agreed upon eight points. They sought no aggrandisement or increase of territory for themselves. They wished no territorial changes which were not requested by the peoples concerned. They respected the right of all peoples to choose their own form of government; and they hoped to see this right restored to those from whom it had been forcibly taken. They undertook to do what they could to ensure freedom of trade and access of all to raw materials. They hoped to further economic collaboration and to secure for the whole world raised standards of living. They desired to establish peace and security after the overthrow of the Nazi regime. They wished to make freedom of the seas available to all. They felt it essential to disarm such nations as threatened the peace of the world, at least pending the establishment of a permanent world security system.

The importance of the Atlantic Charter was later overshadowed by conferences in which the Allies came face to face with awkward practical details. Yet general principles, once solemnly set down, did prove something to aim for in dealing with the Russians or in sorting out the vast accumulation of hatred and misery piled up in Europe. Most remarkable at the time was the fact that the United States, though a nonbelligerent, had set its seal to a document explicitly calling for an overthrow of the Nazi tyranny and expressing willingness to join Great Britain in disarming aggressors and in establishing a "wider and permanent system of general security." Thus at a dark moment of the war and with terrible disasters pending, Churchill and Roosevelt pointed the way to the United Nations and the general principles of postwar settlement.

CHURCHILL came home on the *Prince of Wales* by way of Iceland, where he attended a small parade and one of the countless receptions which warmed his heart. His beaming figure with the cigar and fingers spread wide in the V-for-Victory sign had long been a symbol which people applauded as such; and yet he had never lost his personal touch with a crowd. Everyone cheered him because he was obviously enjoying himself. Pleasure overflowed in his wide smile and jaunty gestures, too unselfconscious for vanity, and always charming because they were sincere. On this occasion, he felt particularly gay to see American marines parading for him and to hear their marching hymn, exactly the sort of stirring tune which he preferred. The Atlantic meeting with Roosevelt had gone extremely well. He was reveling in the sensation of cruising on this tremendous ship, the supreme product of British engineering skill during the last five years. A holiday spirit which had almost gone out of life was again in the air.

Such occasions need to be snatched as they come. At home, the news from Russia was all bad. Stalin was darkly implying that without sufficient help he might collapse. It seemed quite probable that he would be forced to do so if Moscow fell. Meanwhile, the British offensive which was to have cleared the enemy from North Africa hung fire. The build-up there was painfully slow for lack of shipping. And what of the Far East? The War Cabinet and the leader on whose shoulders responsibility hung faced grim decisions.

Aid to Russia was agreed on and probably was vital. Arrangements which had been worked out at the Atlantic meeting could now be put into effect. If, however, the Russians surrendered and all this sacrifice went to waste, what might be expected to follow? Quite possibly the Germans might burst into the Middle East through Persia or into North Africa through Spain. More disquieting even, German roads and railways, built up with painstaking care in prewar years, ran mainly east to west. It would be easier for Hitler to move his forces back to the Channel coast than for Britain to summon her far-flung armies to her aid. If it was not possible to be strong everywhere, should not the strength at home be built up first?

Churchill discounted the notion. The British navy and the Royal Air Force would have to counter this threat as they had done before. The purpose of the army was to seek out Germans and fight them, not sit at home in overwhelming strength. These mounting dangers merely made him anxious to get two more divisions round the Cape and into Egypt, whence they could be moved to Palestine or Persia, or even India if need arose. It had taken available shipping six months to convoy the last division with all of its equipment. What was more, at the moment there were no ships at all which could be spared. But America was in a mood to lend, Churchill to ask, and Roosevelt to comply. Twenty thousand men were taken out in U.S.

naval transports. U.S. freighters displaced a dozen British ships in the North Atlantic, freeing these for the convoy. Within the next five months, the whole huge movement had taken place.

Such a decision, though characteristically bold, was in its essence simple. It agreed on the whole with the views of military leaders. But in the Far East there was no clear-cut answer. In fact, there was really no answer at all; yet something must be done. Japan must soon accept the U.S. terms or fight. It was absolute madness for her to attack the United States, a fact of which the President and his advisers were perhaps complacently aware. Yet though the British and Dutch had followed America's lead in the embargo, they could not be certain that if Japan fell on them alone, America would declare war. In front of the hungry noses of the Japanese troops in Indochina lay Dutch oil, British rubber and tin which they might just possibly have the luck to seize and to keep without being challenged by the one power able to do so. Here was a temptation which might well dazzle the sanest of war lords. It was necessary for Britain to make up her mind what to do and do it at once. Not only were the riches of her fantastic eastern empire at stake, but her relations with Australia likewise. The Australian government had sent an army to Europe which now was in North Africa. It had relied for its own protection on British command of the sea. If this should fail, the bond between the Anglo-Saxon peoples of the British world might for the first time break. Thereafter, nothing would ever be quite the same for the British Empire.

British power in the Far East was naval power and centered on the great base of Singapore in the tip of Malaya. Singapore at this moment was only defended by second-class troops and a hundred and fifty obsolete planes. The modern reinforcements that it needed were going to Russia. By the Naval Disarmament Treaty of 1921, Great Britain had long ago surrendered power to control the Pacific, should she also be involved in a war in Europe. It was thus the opinion of the naval chiefs of staff that for the moment Singapore and the East Indies must fend for themselves and pray for American aid. The best they felt they could do was build up gradually a second-class force based on Ceylon which at least for the time being might protect the Indian Ocean and Persian Gulf from Japanese raiders.

Churchill thought little of this plan. There were the Australians to be considered. America, too, might not view with any pleasure such obvious eagerness to have her do the fighting where British interests were at stake. Besides, so tame a retreat from power was not in Churchill's blood. He insisted with all his usual vehemence that the *Prince of Wales* and the *Repulse,* Britain's newest, fastest, most powerful ships, be sent to Singapore with an aircraft carrier in support. Their very presence might persuade the Japanese that it was wiser to be prudent.

Naval authorities never really liked this scheme; but they felt the political considerations which Churchill pressed on them had weight. Perhaps the battery of his powerful personality was too strong. Perhaps the surrender implied in their own plan was hard for them to swallow. At all events, they allowed themselves to be persuaded. At the very last moment, the aircraft carrier had an accident and was delayed for repair. The others had to sail without air cover. By the first of December, while the Japanese fleet in utmost secrecy steered for Hawaii, the *Prince of Wales* and the *Repulse* had entered the Pacific from the south and were approaching Singapore.

The Japanese sneak attack on the American fleet at Pearl Harbor on December 7th, 1941, was announced to Churchill on that same Sunday evening by a radio broadcast. He called the President at once to confirm the news. It proved to be perfectly true. America at last was in the war. It is hardly surprising that Churchill's first reaction was simply thankfulness. Now victory was certain. Some people pretended that America was soft, but he knew better. England had traversed a long tunnel, and now light shone at the end.

The seriousness of the damage done to the American fleet was not realized at the first, but two days later an Admiralty group met with Churchill to discuss the American disaster and decide how to play the strong card which remained in their hand. The command of the Pacific as a whole was lost; but the *Prince of Wales* and the *Repulse,* both bigger and better and faster than Japanese ships, were still on the spot. If they could make junction with the remains of the American fleet, much yet might be done...

Thus they talked and made their plans. On the following morning as Churchill was lying in bed in his usual way going through dispatch boxes, the First Sea Lord telephoned to inform him that the *Prince of Wales* and the *Repulse* had been sunk by Japanese torpedo bombers. This was a moment, as Churchill himself admits, when he was glad to be alone. In all the ocean from California to the Persian Gulf there was no British or American capital ship. Naked and defenseless lay the riches of the East, lay the settlers of English blood, their wives and children, all their wealth, and the lifework of generations. These must now be swept away. Moreover, the loss of the two great ships was like a blow over his heart. The scheme had been his scheme. His was too rugged a nature to be overcome by vain remorse, yet he needs must know that he had sent them to destruction. He was well aware how many anxious calculations the Admiralty had made in the past two years ... "When the *Prince of Wales* is ready ... when the *Repulse* ... If we can manage until then, we shall be able ..." The loss of one ship of this kind is the loss of an army. It is irretrievable, and the whole course of a war may well be determined thereby. Churchill had learned at the Admiralty to brood over his capital ships with pride and awe. He had got to know them painstakingly one by one. As it so happened, he had cruised on the *Prince of Wales,* dined with her officers, and puttered about asking questions of her crew. He had proudly displayed her to Roosevelt himself. Now she was gone, and all those men that he remembered drowned. As Former Naval Person, his heart mourned for his comrades most sincerely.

He was always especially great in disaster. Never for a moment did he lose his conviction that America's entry into the war was more important than the torrent of catastrophe now rolling on the British Empire. His first reaction had been that he must go to America at once; and he held to this resolution in spite of the invasion of Malaya, the siege of Hong Kong, and all the anxious questions of where to fall back, where to fight to the death, and where one might conceivably hope to dam the flood. He even took with him the First Sea Lord, the Chief of the Air Staff, and Field Marshal Dill, who had till two weeks earlier been Chief of the Imperial General Staff. Thus in the middle of December while perils daily mounted, while the Russian winter set in, and while in the desert their long-delayed offensive was still raging, the leaders of the British war effort handed over their affairs to deputies and set out across the Atlantic.

They traveled on the *Duke of York*, sister ship of the *Prince of Wales*, taking with them vast arrays of office workers and piles of statistics. The holiday atmosphere was totally lacking this time. Everyone was desperately busy, and the weather was grim.

They found America rather a shock. The lavish living, the huge civilian cars, all the signs of wealth and waste appalled these specialists in modern total war. But Churchill liked it. For one thing, he knew America of old; and for another, signs of vigor exhilarated him. He found himself most welcome in the White House, waited on just as he liked, and even provided with an extra room to house his traveling war map. People allowed him to do his business in bed without showing surprise, since Roosevelt's crippled condition had forced him to adopt a similar habit. The two had very free access to each other's rooms; and Churchill, never self-conscious, thought nothing of it when the President caught him in the nude. He was used to receiving in towels, or even without, and to having in people to discuss important matters while he was dressing. He happily did so now while his host looked startled.

He was moved by the warmth of his welcome; but perhaps it had its difficult side. There was too much to do. There were the newspapermen, of course. There was Christmas. He soon was invited to speak before Congress and the Canadian Parliament at Ottawa. Somehow or other these speeches had to be composed; and their delivery with all formalities attendant took up time. Meanwhile, war problems mounted. He ought to get home, but the clear understanding for the sake of which he had made this journey must be established first. He was sixty-seven and had worked at his top speed for over two years. The extra effort was very nearly too much to make; and in trying to open a window in his bedroom, he strained his heart.

American generosity was beyond praise. Churchill was reaping fruits of his past cultivation. His friendship with the President was firmly established, while in the last year and a half he had constantly entertained all sorts of Americans, official or semi-official, and had discussed many kinds of practical problems, including military plans. Chief among these had been a major emphasis of strategy in case the allied nations should find themselves involved in a war with Japan. Both had agreed that Japan by herself was not very formidable, but if she diverted major American strength to the Pacific, terrible consequences might ensue in Europe. Russia might surrender and the Middle East be lost. It was essential that America's main effort should be made first against Hitler while she fought a holding war against Japan.

This decision had been taken beforehand; but in December, 1941, the position looked rather different. For one thing, the blood of the American people was up. They wanted vengeance on Japan for Pearl Harbor, and at once. For another, a holding war without a battle fleet was not too simple. Might it not be wiser to make a gigantic effort before too much was torn away? Considering that by far the greatest losses must be borne by the British Empire, might not Churchill himself have altered his views?

Churchill in fact was far too wise in global strategy to reverse his decision because the war in the Pacific had started badly. He was nervous, however, of the American view and completely relieved to find that the understanding which had been arrived at in former discussions still stood. Both President Roosevelt and General Marshall hastened to reassure him.

Another anxious question remained. British plans for pursuing the war by now depended heavily on American supplies, already cut into by Russian demands. Quite naturally America would need to outfit her own armies. Yet these would not be ready for six months or a year; while in the meantime British troops must do the fighting. Yet again when Churchill prepared to put this view, he found he was met halfway. The Americans really wanted to be allies in the fullest sense and to use their resources intelligently, without jealous national feeling. They also were anxious to learn. They were perfectly ready to set up a Combined Chiefs of Staff on the British model, even though their own organization was still in a primitive state and appeared to the astonished Field Marshal Dill to have descended unaltered from the American Revolution. As American eagerness to co-operate unrolled itself, the vital importance of Churchill's present mission emerged. Differences would be bound to arise later on, and methods of procedure would diverge. The present mood of harmony might have passed if Churchill and his chief military men had not been ready to give it immediate practical expression.

Meanwhile, the conduct of the war brought less satisfaction. Here perhaps the Americans, large-minded but inexperienced, were not the right corrective for Churchill's unscientific dash. His instinct was to be pugnacious in defeat, and so was theirs. He was impelled to make a fight for Singapore, both to please Australia and to give the Japanese a bad time. Troops which might have defended Burma were rushed up to Singapore and lost there. In the meantime, the Americans were anxious to set up a big, over-all command, extending across places isolated by Japanese sea power and no longer capable of real concerted effort. With typical generosity they named an English general for this post, Archibald Wavell. Churchill felt bound to consent, since he had been much deferred to, and after all one's Ally must be allowed to have some views. But this impossible command was powerless to arrest the Japanese, while the defeats it suffered under British generalship did serious damage to England's reputation. Malaya, Burma, the East Indies, all were lost. The tide of Japanese aggression in the next few months swept up to the Indian border, reached out to Ceylon and down to New Guinea, lapping almost to the coastline of Australia. Grimly the military blamed Churchill for some of these disasters, hardly perceiving that his estimate of values was correct. American good will was worth them all.

In general, the military position at this momentous time spread bleak depression in the British high command, who again noticed how Churchill and Roosevelt egged each other on. For the two war leaders were gaily off on a new hobbyhorse almost at once. American relations with Unoccupied France were friendly. It might be possible that French North Africa could be induced to declare for the Allies if given American aid. In this connection, Churchill had very large hopes of the new British desert campaign which as it happened had started just too late to achieve success. Already the victorious British commander was being drained of troops and supplies for the East. His Australian divisions were needed in this moment of peril at home. Meanwhile, the German air force, largely grounded by winter conditions in Russia, had sent reinforcements to dominate the Mediterranean. German submarines had lately been transferred from the Atlantic. In the course of a very few weeks, Britain's Mediterranean fleet was reduced to three cruisers and a handful of destroyers. As a result, German supplies to North Africa, which had been largely interrupted, began to flow in as British reserves were flowing out. Disregarding these tendencies, and disregarding also the greenness of American troops and the impossibility of finding them transport, the African hobbyhorse rose into the air on wings of colored fancy, bearing the President and the Prime Minister agreeably aloft. The fact that these dreams later on came true did not justify their being pressed now while sober men were desperately fighting to save situations almost beyond saving. It was a relief to military feelings when the leaders turned to something broad and general in the purely political sphere, a declaration in the widest terms of their alliance.

For a year Great Britain had fought substantially alone. Now, six months later, she had acquired as allies America, Russia, and China. Numerous nations which had been occupied against their will had governments in exile and were nominally at war. All this had grown up haphazard and might at a peace conference cause confusion. This seemed an appropriate moment for a formal alliance of what were henceforward called at Churchill's suggestion the United Nations, twenty-six in number, including as separate states the British Dominions. Roosevelt and Churchill drew up the text, a declaration of adherence to the principles of the Atlantic Charter and an undertaking to wage war with full resources and not to make a separate peace. These articles were signed by the principal powers on New Year's Day, 1942. It was rather disconcerting to learn a few days later as a result of a visit of the Foreign Secretary to Moscow that Russian adherence to the Atlantic Pact did not mean that she desired no increase of territory or that territorial changes should in her view express the wish of the people. For while Germany was fighting in the West, Russia had annexed the Baltic States. These were for the moment in German hands; but after the war, Stalin made clear that he intended to have them.

This difficult contretemps cast a very slight shadow on the pleasures of the next few days. Solicitous American friends, backed up by Churchill's doctor, insisted on a rest. The loan of a pleasant house at Palm Beach was pressed upon him. The White House muzzled the press while Winston recuperated for five days in the sea and in the sun. To be sure, he was on the telephone to Washington and to England, received or sent out important telegrams, and drew up a long paper on the state of the war at the present time and what was in prospect. To a man of his habits, such activities scarcely amounted to work. He wallowed happily in the shallows and came out refreshed. The peculiar fluttering in his heart very quickly died away. It was a real holiday, but in a day or two he must start home.

He was to have sailed on the *Duke of York* from Bermuda, but set out to join her in a Boeing flying boat, where he fraternized with the pilot, wanted to see all the gadgets, and took the controls for a bit to get the feel. He landed quite convinced that it would be easy and safe to fly to England. Atlantic crossings by air were reasonably common, though less so in winter, when there was agreed to be a certain risk. The Air Chief Marshal looked grave, but was placated by offer of a seat. He, too, was in a hurry. The doctor's objections were forestalled by his being included as well. In other words, Winston had made up his mind; and after the refreshment of a full five days at the beach, it was going to be difficult for anyone on earth to change it. Meanwhile, the weather, which might have vetoed the whole scheme, seemed favorable. Churchill got his way, found his voyage a delightful extension of the

Bermuda trip, ate, drank, and slept with gusto, and landed in excellent spirits. But there had been some risk. Flying through mist for ten hours and in radio silence, the captain got off his course and only decided to turn north just in time to save his cargo from crossing the German batteries at Brest. This brought the plane in from the wrong direction and caused it to be reported to British Fighter Command as an enemy bomber. Six Hurricanes were ordered out to shoot it down. Luckily they missed it, presumably not expecting it to land at Plymouth. Winston cabled to Roosevelt that he had had an uneventful flight with a following wind.

He landed to face a rising storm in England. Amateur critics in Parliament or the press had long been urging Great Britain to be strong in every direction, to open a second front in France, beat Rommel in the Desert, send vast air squadrons to Russia, and build up forces in the Far East which could restrain the Japanese. These optimists had suffered a rude shock, and worse ones were to follow. Far from being strong everywhere, England was to show herself everywhere weak. Already the victories in the Desert had come to a halt as reinforcements were rushed to the Far East. The British people, accustomed for two hundred years to rule the seas, viewed their losses in the Pacific with a sense of growing outrage. After fighting, after toiling as never before for a year and a half, were they still to fail in ignominious fashion through every quarter of the globe?

People's natural reaction was to blame their government. Not every minister was equally popular with the press or every department equally guiltless of muddle. It was being suggested that Churchill, magnificent though he still was, had too much to do. He was getting old, and his load as everyone knew was superhuman. Let him appoint someone as Minister of Defence and confine himself to the political side of the war, to treaties, speeches, and loftily presiding over the national scene. Let him in fact become a figurehead.

This plausible suggestion never had the slightest chance of success, since Churchill had no intention of presiding over a war he could not run. It was, however, taken up by the foreign press and seemed to indicate that Churchill's position was no longer secure. As it was obvious to all those in the know that serious defeats lay ahead, the temper of England was naturally expected to change for the worse. It would be prudent for Winston to rally his forces at once and seek for a trial of strength.

Such a trial could only take place in Parliament. Accordingly, a three-day debate on the course of the war was opened by Churchill with a tremendous speech which took two hours to deliver. This summary of the world situation had to be composed in the two weeks after he came back home and in a period when business of every sort was desperately urgent. Nor was a Churchillian speech ever written for its author and revised thereafter by him, after Roosevelt's fashion. He still shaped the whole himself, most frequently in bed amid a welter of dispatch boxes and other business, breakfast beside him, cigar in mouth, telephone handy, bell constantly summoning stenographer, aide, valet, or scheduled visitor. His rolling periods were tried out in his bath, which he usually ordered long before he had time to get in, though he always expected to find it as full as he liked and with temperature perfect. He would lie there turning the hot tap on with his toes and booming at Parliament, sometimes dictating a section which he liked through the half-open doorway. Not infrequently he would return to the matter in hand at the end of a long day of other business. He would look at a movie for an hour at one in the morning while apparently his mind was still at work. Thereafter, he would pick up a sandwich or a nightcap and walk up and down, muttering new paragraphs to himself, voice occasionally rising into a familiar roar. And so to bed at three, while his secretary stayed up to type the draft.

In such a fashion Churchill composed a speech, dictated it, revised it, had it checked by his private secretaries for accuracy of fact, inserted new ideas, revised it again, and finally allowed it to be typed in what he called speech form — a kind of flowing free verse from which he found it easiest to deliver. He did his tremendous job at high pressure, and this not merely when his speech was vast. The fact was, Winston was still nervous on the days he had to speak and still unable to bring himself to compose until the deadline was ominously near. His stenographers invariably had to work all night before a big speech, and on several occasions they actually went with him down to the House of Commons. There, while he listened to the debate, they were furiously working to type his draft in speech form and would send it into him in the Chamber without even having had time to check for errors.

These methods of work demanded perfect service. One of the secrets of Churchill's enormous productivity was that he understood how to get exactly that. He expected, for instance, to dictate on any subject without warning, always with a cigar in his mouth and very often in a noisy train or plane, or in a car with siren going. Notwithstanding, he must be heard correctly and never, never questioned. His own exuberance might lead him to address a cheerful remark to his stenographer's profile. He did not, however, require conversation. If she responded, he snapped her head off at once for wasting his time. When he looked up from his papers and said, "Gimme this" or "Gimme that," he expected to receive it, notwithstanding the fact that no one had known what subject he was currently engrossed in. On one occasion, he picked up the phone to his private secretary and said imperiously, "Gimme the moon." In the shortest possible time, he was supplied with a list of the moon's phases for the period covering the likely dates for D-Day. He accepted this with no surprise, since it happened to be what he needed.

His office workers slaved for him because their task was desperately important, but also because they admired him at close range and even liked him. What if he treated them all more or less as machines? He was desperately busy, and he had far too many people to see and to consider. What if he jumped on them for the slightest fault? He must vent feelings somehow. No one in the world had more to bear. Then quite occasionally he would say or do some generous thing which made all effort worth while. Men and women worked a twelve-hour day, and very much longer on occasions like the present when a tremendous review of the war impended. Their reward was to see Churchill go off almost on time, manuscript in hand, keyed up and beaming at his public, while they settled down again to catch up with the details of his household expenditure, his constituency, or presents from members of the public ranging from boxes of cigars to a lion.

Churchill's present speech of January, 1942, was frank, detailed, and met criticism point-blank. "If we have handled our resources wrongly, no one is so much to blame as me. If we have not got large modern air forces and tanks in Burma and Malaya tonight, no one is more accountable than I am. Why then should I be called upon to pick out scapegoats . . . ? Many people . . . begin their criticisms and articles by saying, 'Of course we are all in favour of the Prime Minister because he has the people behind him. But what about the muddles made by this or that Department . . . ?' But I am the man that Parliament and the nation have got to blame for the general way in which they are served, and I cannot serve them effectively unless, in spite of all that has gone wrong, and that is going to go wrong, I have their trust and faithful aid."

He followed with a complete and candid exposition of Great Britain's present position, the reasons for it, the defeats to come, and his own certainty of victory with the aid of the United States. Criticism was overborne by the facts so impressively presented. The House was so clearly behind Churchill that it was difficult to find any group to propose a motion against him. Churchill, however, had set his heart on being publicly sustained by a definite vote, and fortunately a way was found to bring one about. Thus at the moment of Britain's lowest ebb, and after the fullest debate, Parliament declared its confidence in Churchill by 464 to one. In the face of disaster, the sentiment of England was still solid.

CHURCHILL had vindicated his government triumphantly, but like a good politician, he spent the next weeks making ministerial changes. Defeats were in the offing. Criticism, if it were not forestalled, would rise again. Churchill lessened the size of his War Cabinet, organized a Ministry of Production on an American model to make co-operation simpler, and found a position for the influential figure of Stafford Cripps. Some less successful ministers lost their jobs, while others of minor importance were elbowed out to make room for better claimants. By resigning the leadership of the House of Commons, Winston even made a nominal concession to those who had said he was too busy — though in fact his deputy had done the work.

These adjustments were being made throughout the month of February, during which the greatest military disaster of British history fell upon her Eastern Empire. Singapore with eighty-five thousand British soldiers surrendered. A defeat on this scale meant more than the loss of a town or an army. It was a portent. In the East, the subjects of England were counted in their hundreds of millions. British mastery was a legend established generations before and never challenged in the memory of the living. It would have been better for England to have abandoned Singapore for a while than to have fought for it, hung out the white flag, and lost an entire army. The whole East stirred.

Responsibility for the defense of Singapore rests on many shoulders, but ultimately — like everything else — on those of Churchill. Great pressure was put on him by Australia to fight for it, and he naturally passed this on to his chiefs of staff. He was himself for a long time under the illusion that Singapore could be held. Always the center of British defense plans in the Far East, it had been fortified between the two World Wars at vast expense. Since, however, it was protected by the whole of British Malaya and French Indochina, there had seemed no necessity for forts on the landward side or fixed guns suitable for bombarding trenches. It so happened that Churchill was unaware of this vital fact, which as he freely admits he ought to have known. More strangely still, he seems to have imagined that a city of a million, a melting pot for all the races of the East, would resist with the dedicated courage of London or Stalingrad. Nor did he ever face the problem of how to supply Singapore after losing command of the sea. By the time that the true situation was understood, the British forces were too heavily engaged to be withdrawn. A last-minute effort to rescue key personnel was unavailing.

The loss of Singapore was swiftly followed by the loss of the East Indies and of Burma. Rangoon fell, and the Japanese swept along the shores of the Indian Ocean. Across the great gulf lay India, already for many years restive. Beyond India lay the oil of the Middle East and a possible junction of the Japanese and Germans. Here the balance of power might be permanently upset, the war decided.

The ferment of India now gave rise to an almost ludicrous correspondence between Churchill, who had studied the Indian problem for years, and Roosevelt, who had not. On the actual, concrete questions of where England's duty and interest lay, Churchill's views had common sense. India must be and could only be defended by England. To grant independence in a hurry at this time would mean at the best that India would be helpless and confused. More probably she would plunge into civil war. Yet ridiculous as Roosevelt's suggestions appear, they represented a state of mind which was to prove important. What really mattered was not how Roosevelt exposed his ignorance, but the fact that his whole view of imperialism was opposite to Churchill's. The British Empire in Churchill's eyes was not merely a glorious achievement of his race, but a contribution to good government throughout the globe. Roosevelt thought it at its best outdated, and at its worst plainly wrong. Nor was this only an American versus a British view. Had the two war leaders been born on the same side of the Atlantic, they would not for all their likenesses of temperament have been of the same party. Reforming liberal and stout conservative, they looked at each other a little askance now and then, their hackles rising.

There was no question of any quarrel. The faith of the two leaders in each other and their cause remained unchanged. Indeed, though the fate of India and Australia appeared to hang in the balance, the tide was actually about to turn. In early April, the Japanese battle fleet attacked Ceylon. It so far outnumbered the British naval strength that Admiral Somerville retired to the African coast to look helplessly on. With nothing to oppose them, the Japanese swept into the Bay of Bengal and sank a hundred thousand tons of merchant shipping. Another catastrophe appeared in sight, and yet mysteriously the enemy retired and did not return. A significant factor had been their serious losses in air battles over Ceylon which had caused three carriers to be sent home to refit. This in turn tipped the scales four weeks later when a thrust at Australia was met by the United States Navy in the Coral Sea. The battle which followed was inconclusive as a trial of strength, but it stopped the Japanese advance to the south. Finally in June when the enemy made his third great attack, this time to the west, he was defeated with crushing losses in the Battle of Midway. The end of the war with Japan was not even in sight, but reverses were over.

Never had Churchill's position been more difficult than in those early months of 1942 when everything went wrong. Britain's real situation was far less desperate than it had been in 1940, but her mood was less exalted. Chamberlain's government could be blamed for the past then. By now, any muddles were inevitably Churchill's own, and there were many. It seemed that the army was incapable of fighting the Japanese. All its equipment was apparently still second-rate. In spite of the mighty effort which the nation had made in aircraft production, planes in Singapore and elsewhere in the East were obsolete. None of the services were showing up very well, not even the Navy. The *Prince of Wales* had been sent out without air cover.

In February Hitler had transferred the *Scharnhorst* and the *Gneisenau* from Brest to Norway. On a damp, dark, foggy day these two great ships had dashed up the English Channel and in spite of every effort had gone through and made their escape. Not in two hundred years had England felt so insulted. It was useless to point out that the Navy preferred to have these ships in the north, that both had been damaged, that visibility had been exceptionally poor, while a radar-jamming system put into effect by the Germans had been unexpected. Most unluckily torpedo-carrying planes were in short supply, since many recently had been rushed to the Mediterranean to offset fleet losses there. All in all, the episode of the *Scharnhorst* and the *Gneisenau* was really trivial; but it was not felt as such in England. The people were losing confidence, perhaps in themselves, perhaps in their leaders. Certainly Churchill still stood out as the only possible Prime Minister. His popularity with the masses was untouched. Yet discontent was there, though still unfocused.

To a veteran party politician, popular feeling is like the weather to a sailor. It determines his actions day by day. He consults it in every maneuver. Churchill's habit of reading all the leading dailies of every political shade was not interrupted to any great extent by the pressure of war. He might attend Parliament only when he had something to say, might leave most decisions on purely internal affairs to other people. His knowledge of the press was still unfailing. The daily papers inspired a significant proportion of what were known as Churchill's "prayers" because he preferred the old-fashioned "pray" to the modern "please." No minister was safe from these, whether his business included the placing of land girls in decent billets, the weeding out of conscientious objectors, or the zoning of fish. With irritating promptness, Churchill would translate some little paragraph in the press into a written order: Pray do something. Pray report on something at once. Pray spend your precious hours looking into some trivial matter which has happened to annoy some part of the public. With such a habit ingrained in him over the years, Churchill must needs be sensitive to a change in Britain's mood about the war. He did not misunderstand it. The determination to struggle was still there. It was the confidence, the mood of Dunkirk and the Battle of Britain, which was lacking.

A victory was needed. What galled him was that a victory had seemed in his grasp in early December. The Desert Army had beaten Rommel soundly; but when the German air force had come down to batter at Malta and open up the German supply route, the British had recoiled. There had been a setback. Three hundred hard-won miles of North African desert had been lost, three hundred miles of air cover for convoys to hard-pressed Malta. If Malta were lost, then the whole supply battle on which the desert war hung would itself be lost, and with it the Mediterranean and possibly Egypt. By early spring, Malta was in desperate straits. The British position in North Africa was therefore in one sense a dangerous one; and yet in another, victory seemed but one jump ahead. Rommel had been decisively beaten. If only the British could mount another attack while he was still off balance, he might be destroyed, and Malta might be rescued.

None saw this more clearly than Churchill, to whose impatience any pause between attacks was a waste of time. Unluckily the British commander, Auchinleck, was of a different sort. Though courageous and able enough, he seemed to lack that sense which Churchill possessed that the other side has difficulties also. Auchinleck was struggling with the consequences of a general diversion of men and materiel to the Far East. He knew also that Rommel was being reinforced. Thus Churchill seeing the chance and feeling the need for a victory came up against a general who saw the chance of defeat and feared its consequences. The telegrams which Winston submitted to his chief of staff to send out to Cairo grew more and more tactless, and it became increasingly difficult to get him to change them. Alan Brooke did not approve of urging men on the spot to act against their judgment, and he did what he could to control Winston's impatience. Finally Winston telegraphed to Auchinleck to come home and argue things out. Auchinleck flatly refused to spare the time. Brooke reassured the General and tried to calm the sputtering Churchill down. The British army had other able men, but there was no assurance that anybody else in command would do any better. A change made now must bring a certain delay.

Winston fretted and fumed. He was in the mood to take chances, partly because he always was, and partly for the sake of England's morale. He, too, knew that Rommel's reinforcements were coming in faster than the British. Time was a-wasting. More important still, without the North African airfields, Malta must soon fall. He put this point to Auchinleck, who merely answered that by attacking too soon, he might lose Egypt. Winston did not believe this. Besides, he saw that if Malta fell, Egypt would go sooner or later.

This latter point convinced the chiefs of staff. With great reluctance and after trying all possible means to get a convoy to Malta, they took a step unprecedented so far. They ordered their commander to attack against his judgment. They thought it probable that he would resign, but he did not. He merely requested the longest reasonable time to prepare and in fact was nearly ready when Rommel, reinforced and re-equipped, fell upon him.

Auchinleck's attitude may appear too pessimistic, but in all due fairness it must be said that his difficulties were enormous. The British war machine was stalling. The sudden extension of the war was much to blame, as were the convoys to Russia. More sinister and more lethal still were the losses in shipping. Submarine warfare had seemed fairly under control as long as convoys were partly protected by the United States, herself a neutral. The entry of America into the war gave the Germans a free hand. Coastal traffic along the American seaboard was not convoyed, and the U.S. government had omitted to prepare for war by taking precautions or producing needed equipment. Shipping losses rose to astronomical heights and stayed there for many months. The actual convoys were left undisturbed for easier prey, but shortage of shipping

began to lay its stranglehold on the life of Britain. Nor was
this all. American deliveries of weapons were falling short.
As was inevitable, and in spite of her generous offers,
America's own needs were coming before Britain's.

Meanwhile, there was trouble brewing between the two
allies. America was anxious to get down to business.
Roosevelt was optimistic and full of ideas. American planners were inexperienced. The Russians were insisting that
a second front in Europe could be established if the Anglo-
American forces cared to do so. The consequence was that
in early April, Roosevelt outlined to Churchill a definite
scheme. Let them both determine on a full-scale invasion
of France in April, 1943. In the meanwhile, let the British
seize a bridgehead in France this very fall, and let them
hold it through the winter. Losses must be heavy and
England's sacrifice very great, but her reward would be a
quick end to the war.

Such a plan in face of the difficulties of the task was
fantastic. A bridgehead could neither be seized nor held,
while the larger invasion of 1943 was probably doomed for
lack of shipping. Optimistic as Churchill always was about
plans for attack, he knew the bridgehead was folly. He did
not, however, say so because he understood American feelings. It would have been easy to give the impression that
England was afraid or had other axes to grind, as the Russians were hinting. Churchill welcomed the Roosevelt plan
with joy, threw his whole weight behind it, and had it
adopted by the Allies — with the proviso that details still
required a careful study. The anxious Russians were informed by both nations that the Roosevelt plan had been

fully agreed on. The British, however, were cautious enough to add that its execution must depend on what was decided by the planners.

The limited invasion for 1942 had little chance. British planners considered it certain to fail and certain to ruin the build-up for 1943. The more they looked at it, the less they liked it. Thus a serious disagreement between the Allies began to loom up during May, causing Churchill great concern. He understood the skepticism of the war-wise British staff, but he understood also the explosive energy of America seeking an outlet. A powerful party in the U.S. was still anxious to divert American forces to the Pacific. This could be fatal to world strategy, yet it might be done if America felt herself frustrated by England.

It was time that Winston went to Washington again. He would fly over in that nice flying boat with the very same pilot. When they got over land, they could drop under the clouds and see a panorama of the whole New England coast and circle New York. No point in not enjoying the trip. He would take with him his chief of staff to thrash out the problems on a professional level with General Marshall. No sooner said than done. He was off at two days' notice, not even allowing the unhappy Brooke to pick up uniforms thin enough for a Washington summer. Winston's own sartorial problems were easier to handle. He was wearing his light blue boiler suit, joy of American reporters. And for emergencies of every sort, his faithful valet would shepherd along his hot-water bottle, his cigars, the elbow pads he liked for working in bed, his green and scarlet dressing gown with Chinese dragons, his eau de

Cologne, the pad he put over his eyes when he slept in the daytime, and every gadget he thought he might want as well as his wardrobe.

Brooke found himself sizzling in Washington, expressing polite disagreement with Marshall, while all the time he uneasily wondered what his imaginative chief was cooking up. Churchill had gone to Hyde Park, where he was busy suggesting to Roosevelt a 1942 landing in French North Africa as something possible for America to do this very year. In other circumstances, his military chief would have liked this plan. It would release trained forces now tied up in Egypt, and by opening the Mediterranean and saving the long haul around the Cape, it would make available a million tons of shipping. Unfortunately, Churchill liked to combine this operation with a landing in northern Norway which his long-suffering military adviser considered perfectly mad. Nor in any case was Brooke exactly happy about planning North African invasions right in the middle of a British defeat in the desert. Rommel had attacked in mid-June. Decisively beaten, the British were giving way in the headlong fashion which desert warfare imposed. One could only be thankful that they had their lines of six months earlier to retreat to, and their base of Tobruk.

As it turned out, Brooke's instinct proved to have been sound. When Roosevelt and Churchill returned to the White House, a message was brought round to them from Marshall's office. A sudden silence must have fallen on their little group while Churchill took in the contents of that pink piece of paper. It contained the announcement of the sudden fall of Tobruk. This news was as bad as the fall of Singapore. In fact, it was worse. The Desert Army was England's best, her single effort to do more than hold on. For the sake of Egypt, the Far East had been exposed to mortal peril. Now ignominiously the army defending Egypt fled, it surrendered to Rommel. In a very short time, the British headquarters in Cairo were burning their papers and planning to get out. Disaster was here.

Churchill took the blow as he had taken other blows. This was a hard one, the more so because unexpected. He would not believe it at first and telephoned London to have the news confirmed. Once more, the Americans were beyond all praise. Their only thought was to help. Three hundred Sherman tanks were literally taken from American units and shipped to the Middle East without delay. However, it was clearly no moment to discuss North African invasions. Plans reverted to their original state. The American build-up in Britain was to be continued while the schemes for a second front were further explored.

This unsatisfactory conclusion was the only one possible. Not only was the war situation fluid, but to Americans Churchill's position at home seemed insecure. British public opinion had sustained a terrible shock. The defeat in the desert was felt to be, and in fact was the low point of the war. A respectable figure in Parliament now filed a motion of censure against the government which was to be debated on Churchill's return. American papers turned this into headline news, and General Marshall asked gravely whether Churchill ought not to cancel his visit to American troops in training. It might not look well in view of the crisis in England.

Churchill reassured his hosts robustly, went through with his program, and flew home at the scheduled time and not before. The reconstruction of his government three months earlier now proved its worth. The solidarity of his ministers behind him was apparent. The opposition lacked a head and lacked a program. The first critic in the debate put forward the old notion that Churchill was too busy to run a war, and that he needed a Minister of Defence to do this for him. His supporter took the opposite tack and blamed the military chiefs. If Churchill only were allowed to make more decisions, everything would go better. Under leadership thus divided, the motion of censure never really got under way. It mustered only twenty-five votes, a miserable number which merely served to strengthen Churchill's hand. No matter what happened, he was the only possible Prime Minister, and England knew it.

The situation remained most critical. General Auchinleck had relieved his commander in the field and taken charge in person. By doing so, he had saved Egypt by the narrowest margin. During the first week in July, a battle was raging along the last possible line of British defense, sixty miles from Alexandria. In England, tempers were strained. Some of the ministers who had loyally upheld Churchill in Parliament still wanted to find out why the Desert Army had so spectacularly failed. Winston was determined to get to the bottom of this, too. He decided to fly out to Egypt and interfere right in the midst of this most critical battle. In order to do so, he intended to fly through the Mediterranean, which was dominated from both shores by the German air force. Dissuaded from this by a concerted effort on the part of everyone in the know, he vented his impatience with even more aggressiveness than usual. About a week later, the situation in Egypt had been stabilized somewhat. The hard-pressed British army had won a breathing space while Rommel regrouped. Churchill seized this moment to wire to Auchinleck about making an attack, and he began to press his project for an invasion of northern Norway on the Canadians, who, as he hopefully said, were used to the climate.

Meanwhile, American tempers were becoming strained also. Roosevelt's project for the 1942 bridgehead in France had been adopted by both countries early in the spring. It had in the American view been confirmed by Churchill's visit. Yet preparations were not being put in hand, and the British blew colder than ever. American feelings on the matter were blunt. The British had agreed. All their chatter about examining ways and means was merely their method of breaking a promise they had not intended to keep. Now was the moment to thump on the table and get tough. Either play ball, or watch America turn herself toward the Pacific.

This quarrel was thrashed out in the month of July. The British case, though really the stronger, did not convince the American leaders until later on in the war when their experience of the difficulties of their task had been enlarged. What overcame them was not the argument in itself, but the good understanding between Churchill and

Roosevelt. These two had always liked the North African scheme. Their imaginations had played over it when America first entered the war. In his June visit, Churchill had put it to the President again, not only as an outlet for 1942, but also as something that would assist an invasion of France by freeing shipping. The President had seen this, even though Marshall had assured him that such diversions always wasted energy and time. Thus there did exist an alternative plan which was a practical one as long as the British maintained their toehold in Egypt. The bridgehead scheme was finally abandoned. There was to be an invasion of North Africa, to which American energies were now devoted.

The tide had turned, but this was not quite obvious yet. Men hoped, but they still feared. Much confusion remained, especially in Egypt. It seemed most probable that Auchinleck must go. Brooke and Churchill had their eyes on Alexander, who had done remarkably in Burma during these months. They needed also a field commander for the Desert Army, and on this vital choice they were not agreed. At all events, they would go out to Cairo and see things for themselves. Beyond Cairo, there loomed the prospect of a visit to Russia.

There were headshakings over a trip of such length. The Prime Minister's doctor did not like the strain for a man of his age. The Cabinet, meanwhile, did not like the dangers of the flight. Winston refused to be put off and kept his protectors on their toes by putting forward semi-serious plans to mislead spies in Gibraltar by wearing a false beard or disguising himself as an Armenian with toothache.

Meanwhile, with his usual resourcefulness, he got hold of an American Liberator bomber which had been roughly adapted for passenger transportation. In this uncomfortable machine, he found it possible to make a single hop from Gibraltar to Cairo. In spite of the drafts and a hard board bed, he arrived at the top of his form, conferred with everyone, drove round in the dust and the sizzling sun to inspect army groups, lunched in stifling mess tents, and wallowed in the Mediterranean in outright defiance of his doctor. The whole command position from India to Egypt came under his rapid review. Auchinleck was replaced by Alexander. Gott was given command of the Desert Army, but two days later was killed. This made it necessary to resort to Brooke's candidate instead of Churchill's. A telegram to London asked them to rush out General Montgomery.

The Russian visit was even more exhausting. Winston made it in order to explain to Stalin personally why there would be no invasion of France in 1942. The situation in Russia was still most critical. This year, the Germans were driving for the oil of the Caspian, for the gateway to Persia, Iraq, and the Persian Gulf. From this direction, England's hard-pressed armies of the Middle East faced mortal peril, for the oil of the Persian Gulf was even more important than Egypt.

Russian hospitality, if a trifle grim in some respects, was princely. Cake and caviar appeared for breakfast. Vodka flowed at all hours. There was a state banquet lasting over three hours with nineteen courses and an uncounted number of toasts. The table was loaded with incredible quantities of food till eye and appetite alike were stunned. Churchill, who possessed one of the hardest heads in Europe, refused to admit that overmuch was drunk. Less fortunate guests went so far as to call the whole evening a horrible orgy. Churchill's lodging was an elaborate villa, reserved for state guests, whose up-to-date plumbing he admired far more than its spacious air-raid shelter or its fifteen-foot stockade and numerous guards. His various companions found themselves made comfortable in a Moscow hotel with armed men at every door and secret microphones installed throughout.

It is hard to say who got the better of the personal duel between Churchill and Stalin. Each wanted something from the other, but neither was prepared to give much away. Churchill found Stalin extremely able, unsentimental and cold, but not incapable of being almost genial on occasion. It was difficult, however, to rely on his moods, which he seemed to vary according to calculation. Deeply chagrined by the Allied refusal to invade France at once, Stalin was artfully led to despair of all aid, and then presented with the North African plan. Almost immediately he saw its strategic possibilities, impressing Churchill with his readiness to grasp the new situation. He almost warmed to the proposal, seemed if not enthusiastic, certainly approving.

Next day the two met again at a larger conference with several of each party present. Possibly Stalin had laid the matter before his council, whose comprehension had not been equal to his. It is also possible that he merely thought he might gain by being rude. For rude he was, not loudly or vehemently so, but in his deliberate, low-voiced, unemotional manner. Speaking apparently more to than through his interpreter, he demanded when were the British going to start fighting. They ought to try it sometime. When they got used to it, they would very likely find it was not so bad. This was too much for Churchill, who had never forgiven the Russians for standing aside during the crisis of the war. Slamming the table, he left his interpreter far behind while he told Stalin exactly what he meant by fighting and a few other home truths as well. Stalin grinned and remarked that he did not understand the words, but liked the spirit. He did not, however, recede one inch from his chosen position, which was that the British had promised a second front in France, which alone could relieve Russia. The Western Allies were deliberately standing aside while Russia did the fighting. From time to time as opportunity offered, he made more offensive remarks in the same unemotional manner. Churchill, however, had made his point and did not intend to work up a quarrel. He remained obstinately bland and pressed the merits of the North African plan.

From these positions, once taken up, neither receded. Each, however, did scan the other and try to make him out. It was Churchill's intention to get to know Stalin with the idea of establishing some basis for mutual trust. This was probably hopeless. Each had his separate past and worked for a different future. One thing, however, they did have in common. Both were fighters. It helped them, moreover, that their habits of life were somewhat similar. Indeed, Churchill, who had exhausted so many in his time, on this occasion met his match. He went to take an official farewell at seven in the evening, for he had to get up before four to catch his plane. To his surprise, Stalin asked him back to his own rooms for a drink. They walked through the Kremlin to the private suite of four rooms in which Stalin lived. Drinks flowed, as usual. Marshal Voroshiloff was invited, and course by course in a somewhat casual fashion dinner appeared. The three men grew quite jolly, chaffed each other through their interpreters, and touched amicably on the troubles of the past. Stalin was only once rude, but that was over a convoy which had lately run the gantlet of surface ships, submarines, air attack, and perpetual daylight, and had been almost totally lost. The Former Naval Person answered politely, but he neither forgave nor forgot.

The evening wore on. Some time after one in the morning, they sent for the Foreign Office representative to draw up an official release for the press about their meeting. Stalin excused himself briefly at two in order to get the latest news from his battle fronts. He had assured Winston that the Caspian and the Caucasus would be held. In fact, in a moment of supreme confidence he actually admitted that a great counterattack was shaping up. About two-thirty, Stalin came back and really started his dinner, which he had only picked at up to the present. Winston excused himself from joining in. The party had gone on now for about seven hours, during the whole of which time it had been necessary for him to keep his presence of mind and speak with caution. Somewhere in the evening he had developed a raging headache. He was finally able to get home in time to bathe and change before leaving for the airport. He slept on the journey, and when he got to Teheran, he canceled the conferences he had intended to hold there and spent a whole day resting.

The situation in Egypt had changed during the short time they had been away. Monty had taken over. He had already toured the battle front, interviewed his corps commanders, issued new orders, and made his plans for meeting Rommel, who was expected to attack again in less than a week. Montgomery's self-confidence was combined with a grasp of the situation which both Churchill and the professional, Brooke, found impressive. The Eighth Army found it impressive, too. Its morale seemed quite transformed. In the circumstances, and with a battle daily expected, Churchill could hardly bear to go away. He did not exactly envisage interfering with Monty. It was merely beyond him to turn his back on the excitement and go home. Brooke was scandalized. The Army had never forgotten how Winston had flown out to Antwerp in 1914 and taken charge. By herculean efforts, Brooke got Winston onto a plane just in time. Behind him, Rommel made his attempt to pierce the British lines and failed. The initiative was passing from the hands of the Axis once and for all, both here and elsewhere.

In January, 1943, President Roosevelt and Mr. Churchill met again for a conference at Casablanca. The various photographs taken of Churchill in the bright North African sun show his expression as jauntier than ever. Well it might be. While the British Eighth Army chased Rommel back across the desert, and while the Western Allies cleared French North Africa of German forces, the Russians had been winning their first tremendous victory at Stalingrad. From this time onward, German strategy becomes defensive in East and West alike. It is for the Allies to plan and execute blows; for the Axis to parry.

This long-expected moment came to Churchill after more than three years of war and when he was sixty-eight. It was remarkable how little he had aged under strain. To be sure, the collar button concealed under his bow tie must now more frequently be left undone to spare the thickening neck. The sparse hair on his vast, domed forehead had lost all trace of red and was now white. The stooping shoulders which the Boers had noticed over forty years ago were very pronounced. He slumped in his chair and let his stomach protrude as he relaxed. But the square, determined face, half bulldog and half baby, was as alert as ever. The trotting walk, the lunging movements were still sudden. Above all, his mind was as clear, his repartee as sharp, his energy as fantastic as it had always been. Yet amid the bodyguard, the valet, the aides, secretaries, and other attendants whom he had accumulated with the passage of time, there appeared also and had done for the past full year the figure of his doctor.

His friendship with President Roosevelt was as warm as ever, but there were new problems. Their relationship with liberated Frenchmen raised the first of many questions which must be answered in liberated Europe. General Giraud was the American protégé, General de Gaulle that of England. It was by no means certain which would have more influence in France. In the meantime, they were not on speaking terms and could only by the direst threats be induced to pose together with the President and the Prime Minister on a Casablanca lawn. Churchill beamed suitably for the occasion, but he was perfectly conscious that the freedoms guaranteed by the Atlantic Charter would not prove easy to agree about. Very possibly the Russians also foresaw trouble ahead. They were taking advantage of their improved military position to be even rougher and ruder than ever. They had actually gone so far as to refuse a medical unit which had been dispatched to nurse the British wounded in the convoys reaching Murmansk.

Meanwhile, the problem of the next move presented itself. General Marshall had been perfectly right when he told the President that diversionary schemes took far more time and effort than ever was foreseen by their backers. In this case, Hitler had decided to fight for Tunisia and had flown over huge reinforcements at great cost. All this time, German submarine warfare kept shipping in short supply. Pacific operations made unexpected demands on landing craft. For all these reasons, an invasion of France in 1943 began to look remote. Churchill was not disposed to hurry it on. He still took for granted that victory over the Axis must be won in France, but he could not resist the tempting prizes now dangling in front of the Allies in the Mediterranean. Italy, never strong, was highly vulnerable to invasion. Greece and Yugoslavia, held down by Italian troops, were already infested by brigand partisans. Turkey, still controlling the Dardanelles and the easy route to Russia, was certainly friendly to England and might be induced to join in the war. Churchill had always wanted to fight everywhere at once, and this was his moment.

These views of Churchill's had not by any means fully developed as long as the situation in North Africa was fluid. Nevertheless, they formed a subject of dispute between him and the Americans which was destined to grow in importance. To Marshall, and indeed to all the American generals, an invasion of France was the immediate goal. Southern Europe was a temptation, a potential waste of troops, and a political involvement which alarmed them. Having no interests of her own in the Mediterranean, America was by no means concerned to fight for Britain's. She was rather disposed to leave Greece and Turkey alone, and preferably Italy too, while she grappled with the Germans.

Such an attitude on the Americans' part suited Russia. British prewar interests in Turkey or the Balkans could be nothing but a hindrance to Russian advance in Eastern Europe. Thus while Stalin continued to press for a second front in France, he constantly derided other efforts. Immediately on leaving Casablanca, Churchill flew to Cairo, thence to Cyprus, and back to Tripoli and Algiers, now headquarters of the Allied armies. Stalin watched his peregrinations somewhat grimly and showed his dislike of the conference with Turkey. In spite of the advantages of opening the Dardanelles, he preferred Turkey neutral to seeing her too intimate with Britain.

Thus from the moment that the initiative rested with the Allies, their disagreements began to emerge. Contrary, however, to the suspicions of the Russians and of some Americans, Churchill's desire to exploit the Allied position in the Mediterranean was as yet less political than purely military. He was not aspiring to bolster up England as a world power by Eastern conquests in Greece or Turkey or the Mediterranean islands. The shape of the future was by no means clear to him yet. He was merely knitting up old friendships or bringing hope to beaten allies.

Neither the Cabinet nor Churchill's doctor had been prepared for this great trip right after the conference at Casablanca. Churchill had as a matter of fact motored with the President to the Moroccan beauty spot of Marrakesh, where he intended to paint and to enjoy the Atlas Mountains. Roosevelt, however, left early next morning; and Churchill felt restless. He climbed back into bed and sent for his commander-in-chief, who had been about to take a well-earned day off in the mountains. Brooke's account of this occasion is worth quoting.

I had frequently seen him in bed, but never anything to touch the present setting. It was all I could
do to remain serious. The room must have been Mrs.
Taylor's bedroom and was done up in Moorish style,
the ceiling was a marvellous fresco of green, blue,
and gold. The head of the bed rested in an alcove of
Moorish design with a religious light shining on either
side; the bed was covered with a light blue silk covering with 6-in. wide lace *entre-deux* and the rest of the
room in harmony with the Arabic ceiling. And there
in the bed was Winston in his green, red and gold
dragon dressing-gown, his hair, or what there is of it,
standing on end, the religious lights shining on his
cheeks, and a large cigar in his face . . .

He greeted me by telling me that we were off at
6 P.M. I replied that I was under the impression that
we had come here for him to paint the scenery he had
been longing to get at for the last six years. He said
he would paint two hours in the afternoon and that
we should start at 6 P.M. I drew his attention to the
fact that even he could not hope to do justice to the
wonderful effects of palm trees and snow peaks in
two hours. He replied again, "I am off at 6 P.M." by
way of clinching the argument. I then said, "All right,
if we are off at 6 P.M., where are we going?" His answer was typical. "I have not decided yet." [1]

Thus began and thus ended Winston's only painting holiday of the war. Yet as usual impatience and impulsive

[1] Quoted from the diaries of Field Marshal Lord Alanbrooke, published in *The Turn of the Tide* by Sir Arthur Bryant. New York:
Doubleday and Co., 1957.

change of plan were on the surface. Underneath them, he was steadily pursuing a definite purpose. For days he had been pressing the Cabinet by telegram to give consent to his going to Turkey, and he was now expecting a final answer. Suddenly his feelings got the better of him, and he determined to set out with the Cabinet's good wishes, or else to go home at once.

He departed with two planes. His personal attendants now numbered nine, while the commander-in-chief had modest claims on a single secretary. His tour included besides the two days in Turkey, discussions in Cairo, a reception in Cyprus, a review of the British army in Tripoli, and a meeting in Algiers. It was in fact a nonstop succession of speeches, interviews, long trips by plane, and constant readjustments to grasp a new situation. Coming on top of the Casablanca conference, it was too much. It was not, however, until he got back to an English February that Churchill fell ill. Characteristically he refused to take much notice and presided over the regular Cabinet meeting despite a cold, sore throat, and fever. Two days later he was known to have pneumonia and was fighting with his doctor because the flow of papers had been reduced to a trickle. Mrs. Churchill, whose quiet intelligence had never taken nonsense from her husband, now lent her influence to maintain order. The Prime Minister, complaining loudly of idleness and boredom, was induced to read a novel. He felt very ill for about a week, but his constitution triumphed as usual. The flow of papers and visitors was soon resumed. It was noticeable, however, that even in May when a trip to Washington over the Italian situation loomed up, his

doctor flatly refused to let him go over by air, and he had
to resort to the *Queen Mary.*

Great precautions were taken to deceive spies, for preparations to receive him on a troopship in wartime were
elaborate. For one thing, the *Queen Mary* was lousy.
Coolies at Suez had brought their vermin aboard, and there
was now nothing for it but to gas her and trust that till the
hatching of the next set of eggs, she would be habitable.
Her whole interior as a luxury liner had been stripped.
To accommodate the British chiefs and their office staff
much work had to be done, which spies would notice. Accordingly, the suites were fitted up as though for the Queen
of Holland, with pictures to match. To confuse rumor,
ramps were carefully built everywhere to foster the suspicion that the President of the United States would make a
return visit on this ship. It was known that a special agent
had been sent to Algiers to murder Churchill on his recent
visit. Spies constantly watched for his going and coming
through Gibraltar. On his very next trip, they perceived
a thickset man with a cigar take off in the regular neutral
passenger plane and notified the Nazis, who shot it down.
It can hardly have seemed likely that Churchill would
travel in this way, but any chance was worth the taking.

This was a year of conferences. No sooner did Churchill
get back from Washington in June than another meeting,
on the largest scale, was planned for August in Quebec.
The Anglo-American struggle for control over policy was
reaching a climax. The British intention was to knock
Italy out of the war, by this means diverting large German
forces from their main fronts to southern Europe. The

Balkans, for instance, were held down by Italian troops.
Hitler must either replace these or let the Balkans go if
Italy surrendered. Unhappily, the Americans regarded
such ideas with great suspicion. The original invasion of
French North Africa had certainly resulted in great success
for the Allies. It had duly opened the Mediterranean and
eased the pressure on shipping. It had, however, played
its part in postponing an invasion of France till 1944. The
Americans suspected that an attack on Italy was being put
forward as an excuse for avoiding next year's cross-Channel
operations. They preferred to pull in their horns and do
nothing. Meanwhile, on the other side of the world, positions were reversed. Here it was the Americans who
wanted an aggressive war, the British a holding one. England was pressed to open a costly jungle campaign and to
re-establish contact with China.

Many Americans have suggested that Churchill never
cared for the cross-Channel attack. This is unfair to him,
and even ungrateful, considering that he inspired the artificial harbors which the Allies used to supply their troops
until Cherbourg could be used. However, it is perfectly true
that the number of his projects would in itself have made
the cross-Channel invasion impossible, had they all been
carried out. His Chiefs of Staff Committee strove as val-
iantly to keep his imagination in bounds as he did to en-
large theirs. Americans, however, could never be quite sure
how far the ideas he put forward agreed with those of his
advisers, how far not. They ran the risk of taking seriously
some scheme which came to nothing. At the moment,
for instance, Churchill did not believe in the jungle cam-

paign or the virtues of Chiang Kai-shek's China. He reacted by developing an obsession for the southern tip of
Sumatra which annoyed his commander-in-chief almost as
much as northern Norway. When Winston got into these
moods, he sourly reflected, no consideration of available
landing craft or even of the next strategic move could ever
shake him.

It was the good understanding between Churchill and
Roosevelt which had hitherto resulted in England having
the last word on strategy in Europe. This could not continue. Very naturally, as the President's advisers pressed
their views, or even their suspicions, Roosevelt's attitude
hardened. His personal friendship for Churchill remained
warm. It does seem probable that Roosevelt's humor did
not amuse Churchill very much. Both determined talkers
certainly thought the other monopolized the conversation.
All the same, each was impressed by the other's real abilities. Mrs. Churchill came over for the conference at Quebec, and both she and her husband went down to visit at
Hyde Park. However, the British contingent found the
Quebec discussions far from easy. It is true that for the
moment the situation favored their view. Italy had fallen
like a ripe fruit before it was touched. Mussolini had been
deposed and arrested in July. The successor government
was only anxious to surrender, provided the Allies would
appear in sufficient strength to drive out the Germans. In
these circumstances, an Italian campaign was unavoidable.
All the Americans could do was restrict its scope and insist that nothing whatever should interfere with the pace
of their build-up in England.

Unluckily, at the time of the Quebec conference, the task of the Allies in the Mediterranean looked easier than it turned out to be. They had reckoned without the peculiar temperament of Hitler. Knowing as they did that German resources were now stretched to the utmost, they did not imagine that he would attempt to take over not only Italy itself, but Greece and all the islands which Italian garrisons held in the Aegean. Gratifying though this certainly was in a way, it meant that larger forces might be needed by the Allies than had been assigned. In the Aegean, for instance, possession of the islands depended on taking Rhodes, which was well fortified and now in German hands. Middle East command had shipped most of its equipment to Tunisia or the Far East and needed nine LST's from somewhere or other in order to take Rhodes. Accordingly, Churchill applied to Roosevelt for these. Considering the resources of the Allies even at this point, his seems a modest request. Its timing, however, was most unfortunate. Hardly had the forces of the alliance been allocated to the various fronts, at the cost of long discussions, than Churchill demanded this change. By now the Americans were convinced that he always would demand a change, and that to the British, agreement only meant a point of departure. Roosevelt refused. In fact, he persisted in refusing, despite all the pressure which Churchill knew how to apply. Rhodes was not captured. British garrisons which had taken over islands elsewhere were wiped out by the Germans at leisure. Turkey stayed neutral, and British prestige in the Middle East suffered a shock.

This experience was a bitter and humiliating one for

Churchill, but it completely failed to teach him a lesson. Almost immediately he began to press for landing craft for Italy. It had been the Allied intention to form a line north of Rome and stand there on the defensive. They had not reckoned with the confusion of the Italian collapse or the aggressiveness of Hitler. It soon became obvious that a campaign would have to be fought south of Rome in the Apennine Mountains, where every advantage of terrain was with the defender. The obvious answer was to make a series of landings on the coast and outflank German lines as fast as they could be formed. To do so, however, would cause a delay in the cross-Channel invasion, now scheduled for May 1, 1944. The smaller landing craft, once sent to the Mediterranean, could not return across the Bay of Biscay during the winter season. They must be left till spring, and D-Day must wait their convenience.

Perhaps it was true that a postponement of D-Day by one month or even two was not important. Certainly, however, it was tactless of Churchill to associate himself with a further delay. He merely sustained another rebuff and confirmed the opinion which the Americans had that he disliked the cross-Channel invasion. Though in fact some landing craft were sent to Italy in the end, the bad impression which Churchill's arguments had made was never effaced.

This difficulty overshadowed the last and largest conference of the year, that of the Big Three at Teheran, which was preceded and followed by an Anglo-American meeting at Cairo. Churchill was not well. He came out by ship through the Mediterranean with a cold and a sore throat nothing would shake. He spent the voyage in bed, and when he got to Malta, his strength sufficed for nothing but a tour of the bomb damage, which he felt that he must make somehow if he could so much as stand on his feet. He arrived at Cairo feeling slightly better, and with the aid of all his doctor could do, he was able to carry on. However, fatigue produced a relapse, and by Teheran he was almost speechless and entirely dependent on gargles to keep him going. His constitution was giving way under strain at last. His sixty-ninth birthday came up at this very conference at Teheran.

Churchill had hoped that before the Big Three meeting, points at issue between himself and Roosevelt might be thrashed out. From the beginning, however, affairs took a difficult turn. The President had invited Chiang Kai-shek and Madame Chiang to Cairo, with the result that the Far Eastern question, which Churchill would have liked to avoid, dominated the meeting. The political relation between Churchill and Chiang Kai-shek was cool. The Chinese general aspired to pose as a native Asian leader in a Far East dominated by England. He had accordingly at the height of the Japanese peril communicated with Indian nationalists and expressed himself unhelpfully and critically about the defense of Burma. Churchill had not forgiven these episodes, which had galled him all the more because he did not believe in Chiang's pretensions. He was aware that the General's empire in China was rickety, that his administration was a bottomless sink of corruption, and that he faced perils not only from Japan, but within China.

It was therefore with determined opposition, almost with resentment, that he met Roosevelt's desire to elevate Chiang to the status of a partner on equal terms with the Big Three. However, say what he would, Churchill could not deny that Chiang had claims to notice. He was for one thing anti-Communist. He had struggled for years against Japan and was somehow containing a major part of the Japanese land army. More important still, he was in possession of an area whence Japan could be bombed. What Roosevelt wanted was for the British to recover Burma, reopen the Burma Road into China, and pour supplies through it to set up air bases where needed.

Churchill thought this plan all very well, but the difficulties of campaigning in Burma on a big scale were quite enormous. It was still not possible to apply weight everywhere at once. The largest Allied army in contact with the enemy at this time was in Italy. It was four-fifths British. Churchill was unwilling to let this mass of trained troops sit idle while supplies were diverted to a very dubious campaign in Burma. He could not and need not refuse to act at all, but he found himself drawn into tedious arguments which he would rather have avoided. He was therefore horrified to learn that Roosevelt had verbally and without consulting him given Chiang Kai-shek a promise that the British would stage an amphibious assault across the Bay of Bengal on the Andaman Islands.

This was really too much! The precious landing craft which he had been begging for turned out to be available after all and were lightheartedly promised at the other end of the world and for an operation which the British had

not offered to make and did not believe in. British chiefs
were adamant in refusing to undertake it. Americans, however, backing up their President's given word, were equally
insistent that it must forthwith be done. A deadlock impended.

It seems most probable that in the privacy of his quarters
in the British Embassy in Cairo, Churchill went into one
of his royal rages. These explosions were the envy and awe
of all who had the opportunity to hear them and to admire
the rich resources of the Churchillian vocabulary. The
story goes that on his visit to Russia, Churchill had broken
into one of these tirades against Stalin in the privacy of
State Villa Number Seven. Reminded in some agitation
that the place was certainly wired for sound, he deliberately
walked up to every fixture and told it in no uncertain
terms what he thought of everything Russian. After a magnificent display lasting a considerable time, he blew off all
his steam and returned completely to normal, chuckling
over the excitement of the unseen listeners-in. On the
Cairo occasion there were no microphones, and what
Churchill said in the privacy of his rooms is not recorded.
The chances are, he said a great deal. This was not the
first occasion that the President's glib tongue had got his
ally into trouble. At Casablanca, the two war leaders had
given a conference to the press. Roosevelt had spoken first
and had been asked a question in reply to which the
phrase "unconditional surrender" had somehow popped
into his head. He had said it, and in this offhand way
committed the Allies to a policy which they afterwards
felt they must adhere to. Churchill, taken completely by

surprise, had nevertheless backed Roosevelt up. Now, on this second occasion, the Andaman Islands had somehow popped out while the President was exercising his famous charm on Chiang Kai-shek. It was not reasonable that he should commit a friend and ally in this arbitrary fashion.

The President and the Prime Minister went off to Teheran without solving, and almost without discussing their differences in the West. The effect of this was to set up Stalin as arbiter. He was asked whether he preferred an active Italian campaign with some postponement of D-Day or a strictly punctual invasion of Normandy, coupled with a landing which the Americans desired in Southern France. He preferred the latter for reasons which might have been as much political as strategic. It was therefore agreed upon. Churchill found himself in an awkward position which was accentuated by the conference living arrangements.

Each of the principals had originally intended to stay in his own embassy. It happened, however, that the British and Russian embassies were next door, while the American was some way off and on the other side of town. It was clearly dangerous for Roosevelt to traverse daily the narrow streets of Teheran, where security precautions were insufficient to prevent some Axis agent from tossing a bomb. The Russian embassy was larger than the British and contained suitable quarters for Roosevelt as well as Stalin. Accordingly, Roosevelt moved in and took the opportunity to exercise his charm on the Russian dictator. Churchill began to suspect that his own attitude toward the cross-Channel invasion was being misrepresented to the Russians. Now more than ever he regretted the waste of time that

Cairo had been. Stalin had declared himself ready to go to war with Japan after the defeat of Germany, which in itself solved the problem of access to China and of bases for bombing. No misunderstanding with the President over this need ever have arisen.

Churchill did his best to remedy a situation which was daily becoming more difficult. In an attempt to thrash out the problems which ought to have been debated at Cairo, he invited the President to lunch. Roosevelt refused, giving as his reason that a private conference between the two of them would make Stalin suspicious. Considering that the President had not hesitated to lunch alone with Stalin, this seemed unfair. Determinedly, Churchill himself sought a private meeting with Stalin and explained his views. To condemn the large British army in Italy to inactivity for the next five or six months would be foolish and un-wise. Only by attracting large German forces into southern Europe could the defense of France be sufficiently weak-ened to make invasion a success. And with that very same end in view, the German forces in Yugoslavia, Greece, and the Aegean Islands must also be pinned down or increased. In sum, he, Churchill, desired to fight the Germans. Only in Italy were the British at present doing this, and they did not intend to stop what they had started.

This much Churchill said, and it is notable that in spite of everything, he did fairly well in the long run carry his point. Other people, however, had begun to notice that Roosevelt was trying to outdistance his British colleague. Roosevelt prided himself on his influence over Stalin, and it was evident that the Russian was far politer to him than he was to Churchill. The general opinion was that Stalin did not know how to make Roosevelt out. That extraordinary combination of weakness and strength, cunning and naïveté, far-seeing wisdom, vanity, and indiscretion puzzled many, but none more than the tough, cold opportunist. A surface understanding between Roosevelt and Stalin was established, and it led to their joining together to bait Churchill. Too much was made of this. To be sure, Churchill once lost his temper with Stalin and Elliott Roosevelt and stalked out of the room. He had, however, lost his temper with Stalin on his earlier visit; while he thought Elliott, whom he never greatly liked, had been impertinent. Still, the fact was, he made a scene and took public notice of an awkwardness which he might have been wiser to keep to himself. If there was a shadow on his friendship with Roosevelt, it could but be deepened by any public gossip over the issue.

One successful effort for harmony Churchill made. It was his birthday, and he insisted on his right to give a party. It was in his mind that England was a far older world power than the other two, and that in this particular war she had been fighting longer than either. It was not sufficient that he should be the guest of honor and sit in the right-hand seat. He would sit in the middle, and England should be the host. For him, this occasion was the highlight of the conference at Teheran. Sore throat, fatigue, chagrin were put aside for the supreme moment when his personal position could gain an advantage, even of this superficial sort, for England. Nothing marred the occasion. The Russians were always jovial in carousing, and

Churchill understood how to make a party go. A sort of harmony was re-established here which let the conference pass for a success. This was all that mattered.

So much Churchill accomplished. Meanwhile, at Teheran and later again with Roosevelt at Cairo, his slow, persistent negotiations disposed of the Andaman Islands and began to lay the groundwork for the new offensive in Italy and for the amphibious landing behind the German lines at Anzio. He went home via Tunis with the idea of discussing these plans with General Eisenhower, the Allied commander-in-chief. When, however, he arrived at Eisenhower's headquarters, the lingering illness which he had fended off prevailed at last.

It was pneumonia again and the complete collapse of utter fatigue. It was almost too much trouble to lift a hand or turn his head on the pillow. He said he would now read *Pride and Prejudice* and fill in one of the gaps in his deplorable education. The fact was, however, that it was not worth the effort to hold a book, and he had it read to him. His daughter Sarah had luckily been on this trip as his aide; and presently Mrs. Churchill appeared, flown out from England in foggy, unpleasant weather. He cheered up visibly at that and began to get better. Drugs and his extraordinary physique pulled him round, but the doctors insisted on a three-week convalescence before he considered any sort of trip back to England. Everyone was anxious to get him out of Tunis, where he was by no means safe from a long-range air raid or a sneak attack by German submarines. Marrakesh attracted him again, and the villa there was once more at his disposal. The bed with the blue silk cover had been most comfortable! His people got him onto a plane, though he was so weak he hardly was able to walk up the gangway alone.

He spent three weeks at Marrakesh recovering. His long-suffering bodyguard, who had been with him for many years and had learned in the process the duties of valet, errand boy, nursemaid, digger of swimming pools, mixer of cement, and general porter, now committed the supreme folly of a blameless career. Discovering that Churchill had a great desire to see the view from the top of a Moorish tower, the Scotland Yard detective rigged up a chair with handles and assisted to lug Churchill — no mean weight — up a narrow circular staircase which had never been designed with this in mind. The fact was, it was such an enormous pleasure and relief to know he was getting better that had Churchill demanded the sun and stars, it seems most probable that his devoted staff would have somehow supplied them. No one could call him an undemanding employer, yet everybody who served him in any capacity seems to have loved him.

He got home at last in mid-January, having been absent well over two months and ill for more than half. The most important thing in England was the coming cross-Channel invasion. All the difficult negotiations of the past year, if seen in proportion, were not more than incidents in the closest alliance between two sovereign, independent powers that has been known. Its greatest achievement was to be the expedition which puts in the shade all other amphibious operations from the taking of Troy until now. It would not have been possible, had not the administrators

of each country at every level put common interests first
and national feelings a very long way second. This was
particularly important in England, where the troops arriv-
ing from overseas had somehow to be housed, where all
the equipment they brought with them must be stored,
where the hard-pressed civilian labor force must find the
men for countless new installations. Individuals or institu-
tions were dispossessed all over southern England. Chartwell itself was requisitioned for offices. New American
faces appeared every day, many of them belonging to
people who had not met Britishers before and did not know
how to take them.

In these and all other difficulties, Churchill consistently
set the tone. From the very beginning he had got to know
the leading Americans well. His dinner parties, and even
his country weekends were international. There had never
really been any question of using Chartwell himself since
the beginning of the war. He could not afford it, once his
very large extra income from writing or from lectures was
cut off. Luckily, however, the Elizabethan manor house
of Chequers had been left to the nation shortly after the
First World War as a country house for the Prime
Minister to entertain in. No one has ever used Chequers
quite so intensively for the purpose it was designed for
as Churchill did. If Americans after a heavy week found
his late hours appalling, they all sensed his warmth and
felt his magnetism. Nor did the most suspicious ever question his devotion to their common cause, defeating Hitler.

As preparations advanced, Churchill's supervision of the
whole situation in England grew more detailed. He

wanted to be sure that every problem was as far as possible foreseen, that every instance of Anglo-American friction at every level was taken in hand. His "prayers" and his tours of inspection grew more frequent. As far as possible, he wanted to see for himself. In particular, any new and ingenious ideas — and there were many — commanded his interest at once. He wanted to fire things with his own hand, to swim in an amphibious tank, or be instructed what buttons to press and what handles to pull on every object. Characteristically, he found his recreation this way while he was busy impressing his personality on the whole war effort. Thoroughly conscious of his effect on morale everywhere, he used his tours to promote co-operation and care for American troops at every level.

His whole fierce energy was thrown into these preparations. This was an operation of war on a gigantic scale, supremely worthy of his peculiar talents. The temptation to take part in it himself was irresistible. To do him justice, the Prime Minister was not entirely small-boy in his attitude to danger. He was capable of refusing an airplane trip to a lovely oasis because he felt it his duty not to take the risk of flying for pleasure. In this sort of fashion his good common sense did defer to other people's solicitude about him. However, the impulse of his nature was all the other way. While he acknowledged that he ought to take shelter in an air raid, instinct bade him go up on the roof and watch. In the actual presence of danger, instinct far too frequently won; and on every occasion it only gave in with a struggle. It was struggling now. The Prime Minister wrestled with his feelings, or so one may presume; but they were too strong. To the consternation of all who feared for his life or knew his capacity for interfering with generals, he announced his intention of going out with the cruiser squadron to bombard German defenses.

People were appalled. They remonstrated. Churchill responded that he had thought the matter through, not frivolously, and had made up his mind. Men like himself whose business was to send other men into danger ought occasionally to expose themselves likewise. It made them realize the responsibilities of their task. In this supreme moment of the war he of all people had earned the right to be there. He intended to be so.

This specious reasoning failed to convince anybody at all, but the fact did not discourage him. No one was in a position to tell him what to do. In desperation, his advisers appealed to the King.

George VI was not lacking in courage either. In fact, his first reaction to the proposition had been that he would go too. Convinced, however, that he should only be in the way, he unwillingly consented to stand aside and let the professionals do their proper job. Having done so, he found it easier to see what a difficult position Churchill would put the commanding officer in. He appealed to his Prime Minister with an authority which really could not be denied. Churchill submitted, though not with a very good grace. He was not, and never was to be convinced. The expedition to which he had contributed so much and which his leadership of England alone made possible went on its way without him. He had to be content with a visit of inspection as soon as it could be reasonably managed.

People in England lay awake through the night of June 5th, listening to the endless roar of planes departing from airfields large or small throughout their island. Churchill was awake, too; and he went to command headquarters, there to do nothing because there was nothing to do. Eisenhower went to bed. On the tracks of the plotters, ships of all kinds were converging, ships put in motion two days ago from tiny, distant harbors, or ships crowding to the rendezvous from Portsmouth, Folkstone, Dover, whence the flashes of guns on the coast of France were often seen. The men who plotted the weather were sitting up also, watching reports come in from weather stations in Iceland or the Atlantic. No change in conditions could put off invasion now. Parachutes were already falling through the night. Planes had cast off their gliders. People at headquarters might glance at their watches and calculate that in little bits and pieces, round a key bridge here or a key fort somewhere else behind the German lines, the fighting had started.

Churchill went to bed before the dawn. Like Eisenhower, he foresaw a trying day. As the gray mist rolled off the sea and revealed to a German watcher a thousand ships headed his way, the men in England who had set that armada in motion lay asleep.

That day the great naval guns bombarding the Normandy coast could be heard distinctly in England, though scarcely in London, where Churchill was informing his high-placed colleagues who had asked not to be told the day or the hour. He would have been happier aboard, for the jobs that he was busy doing could hardly have lightened for him the strain of waiting. All day the landing ships discharged their endless contents on narrow strips of beach. Men battled and died, and as yet no news came out. No man knew better than Churchill that in a sense this great invasion was the purpose of his whole life. On what might happen in the long hours of this day depended England's future, the course of the whole war, the fate of Europe.

B Y THE MIDDLE of August, 1944, Churchill was back again in the Mediterranean, where, cruising off Naples, he met a great convoy of American troops who were going to make a new Allied landing in Southern France. They lined the rails to cheer him. He waved back with great good will, though he wished they were elsewhere.

Victory in Italy had come at last. It had fallen to Churchill to announce in the very same speech the taking of Rome and the Normandy landings. As a result, the Allied invasion of southern France, which was to have drawn off German troops from Normandy, could not take place in June because the Allies were still too heavily involved in Italy. Immediately, Churchill desired to have this plan changed. The object of their landing in the south of France had very largely been achieved, or so he said, by the attraction of ever-growing German forces to the Italian front. After the annihilation of these, it would be better to let the army in Italy strike up the Adriatic into Hungary and Austria.

The Americans refused to alter their plans. They did not, Roosevelt replied, think it desirable to dissipate their strength in adventures in the Balkans. The answer is interesting because Churchill had neither mentioned nor intended a Balkan campaign. Doubtless the Americans, judging on his past performance, held the conviction that once they gave way at all, they would inevitably by another change of plan be involved in the Balkans. In any case, their strategy had always consisted in putting their entire weight behind one punch. They may or they may not have been right. No one can be so foolhardy as to lay it down as a fact that the Allies would have ended the war more quickly by attacking Germany from the south as well as the west. Militarily, therefore, the American judgment has been confirmed by success. Politically, it has been attacked because of its failure.

With the Normandy invasion, Allied strategy had more or less taken shape. From this time onward, every divergence between the Western Allies was bound to become less strategic and more political. Preliminary outlines of the future had been sketched at Teheran and had looked promising. The three chief signatories of the Atlantic Pact had not been prepared to interpret literally their statement that they desired no annexations. America wanted bases in the Marianas and elsewhere. She had no intention of handing back Pacific islands to Japan. Russia wanted the Baltic States and parts of Finland and Poland which had belonged to her in 1914 and which had proved their strategic value in the Second World War. She also wanted ice-free ports at the expense of Germany or Japan, or even both. England, as it so chanced, wanted nothing. Churchill, however, was far too worldly-wise to lay claim to purer motives than the rest. Wars are created by the suspicions and fears of powerful states as often as by their appetites. A satisfied

Russia and a safe America were England's best guarantees for future peace.

In this unheroic, practical way a good understanding had been reached on preliminary points. Americans now wished as far as possible to leave things there, perhaps for the very good reason that they alone of the three great combatants were not on the spot. Their military leaders were of course operating in Europe, but their government was necessarily somewhat out of touch. It was not possible for Roosevelt to fly over to Italy, as Churchill was now doing, and hold a conference with Marshal Tito of Yugoslavia. Naturally Roosevelt worried lest arrangements be made he could not approve of. He was particularly anxious to avoid setting up any "spheres of influence" in Europe, readily foreseeing that such a process might lead to open partition of countries between the Western Powers and Russia.

Churchill, too, was anxious to avoid a division of Europe; but he concerned himself with things as they were at the present, clearly perceiving that the state of these must dominate the future. It was not practical for Britain and the U.S. to enter a peace conference in a year or two with talk of freedom if in the meanwhile Italy, Greece, Yugoslavia, Hungary, and Czechoslovakia had all gone communist. For the communist parties in those states where the German yoke was entirely or even partly thrown off were trying to profit from the weakness of earlier regimes. The King of Greece had never sat firmly on his throne and had now been in exile in England for over three years.

The King of Yugoslavia, likewise in exile, had been a boy of seventeen when the Germans drove him out. His shaky position had been further complicated by what amounted to a civil war between Croats and Serbs in which the latter had availed themselves of German aid. The hapless King Peter, himself a Serb and perfectly ignorant of what was going on inside his country, had backed the wrong horse. The King of Italy was hopelessly discredited by his long association with Mussolini. Thus various governments which the British had received as allies were not acceptable, or probably not so, to the mass of their subjects.

The obvious answer to all these questions was a plebiscite and a government established by choice of the people. Someone, however, must supervise this. Communist parties were nowhere in the majority as far as one could tell. They were, however, revolutionary by nature, to a very large extent armed, and stimulated by secret Russian support. For friendly though Stalin had been at Teheran, his opportunism would not let him throw away a magnificent chance. The stake he played for was the mastery of Europe, rendered possible by the defeat of Germany and the collapse of France.

Churchill saw this situation very clearly. He had never had any illusions about the Russians, while for nearly thirty-five years European politics had been his preoccupation. To the more distant view of Roosevelt, issues seemed confused. Besides, American thinking was colored to a certain extent by political slogans. Imperialism was wrong. The British were an imperial power. The Russians were a republic and in a classless society, too. Mistaking the shadow for the substance, the American government was trying to shut its eyes to naked imperialist aggression as it sprang up in a new form. American reluctance to become too deeply involved in Europe was a natural cause of this error, as was also another American slogan, which was that wars in Europe are invariably caused by the "balance of power."

It is perfectly true that the balance of power in Europe has been a fundamental principle of its political life since the sixteenth century and has, if one likes to look at it that way, been at the bottom of most of its wars. What America did not stop to think was, granted the balance of power might not be worth maintaining, was the alternative more acceptable? For the alternative to a balance in Europe must be its domination by a single power, which in the postwar world could only be Russia.

As a consequence of these different views, Churchill's popularity in America after D-Day was perceptibly waning. He was still the inspired war leader, yet he was also the old political horse drearily performing the same old circus tricks in a new world. What was all this business of cooking up a deal with Russia, whereby England should have a free hand in Greece and let the Russians do what they liked with Rumania? Churchill defended himself with spirit. England had expended forty thousand lives in fighting for Greece in 1941; had received the Greek government in exile; had Greek forces under her command in the Middle East; and did not intend to allow any band of extremists to establish their dictatorship by force. As for Rumania, Great Britain had no commitments there, and Russia would certainly do what she pleased. It was expedient, however, to make Russia aware that in these matters there must be tit for tat.

Roosevelt agreed because he really had no alternative. His interests, as he was well aware, were fundamentally the same as England's. He did not like, however, this demarcation of spheres of influence; and he was of the opinion that the proper approach to Russia was to trust her. Old-fashioned bargaining only led to mutual suspicion.

All this lay in the background of that chance meeting off the Bay of Naples between Churchill and the American troops now bound for Toulon. No consideration of the expediency of getting a foothold in southeastern Europe had clouded the American decision. Rather they had hastened to dissociate themselves from England's political foothold in the Balkans. For good or for ill, their blows were to be struck in France, while the remnants of the Allied army left in Italy might rest there on their laurels.

Before 1944 was out, these tensions had brought an explosion. Taking advantage of the German withdrawal to strengthen their main fronts, Communist Greek forces attempted to seize Athens and set up a government. Churchill was faced by an awkward decision. British strength in the Middle East was far from adequate to put down Greek civil war. Because of its defeat over Rhodes, the army in Egypt had no bases for a sudden descent on the mainland of Europe. Yet the alternative was a Communist regime in Greece, established against the wishes of the bulk of the Greek population. Churchill's temperament and his sense of policy agreed on sending a token force to Athens in a hurry. Here it found itself unable to defeat the Communists, but just sufficient to prevent them taking control. Battle swayed back and forth in the streets of Athens, while the populace as a whole cursed Communists and cowered.

American newspapers with one accord took up the revolutionary cause. Churchill was a monarchist and two generations out of date. His aim and object was to force on a freed people a pro-British king, a close connection of the British royal house, who had never really been popular in Greece or governed well. It certainly was not for dubious aims such as these that American soldiers were fighting and dying in France. So great was the vehemence of American popular feeling that it seemed as though the moment for which Stalin was waiting had arrived. A rift had opened between the Western Allies which might go very deep. Yet whether from caution or whether from respect for his agreement with Churchill over the Balkans, Stalin refrained from widening the gap. Russian papers remained scrupulously correct and left their partisans in Greece entirely to the British.

The Greek affair sputtered and died out. On a bitter-cold Christmas, Churchill flew out to Athens, where he narrowly escaped death from a bullet which missed him and killed a bystander. In an icy conference room, all light and heat cut off, he met with delegates of both groups and persuaded them to join a temporary government under the regency of Archbishop Damaskinos. This was an admission of Communist failure, yet presumably a guarantee against reprisals. The moderate party was enabled to gather strength, while the King engaged himself not to reappear unless a plebiscite should summon him to do so. Churchill's diplomacy had really scored a success. American opinion caught up with his in time, but for the present suspicions between the two great countries were deepened. Most unfortunately, it was the present which was crucial.

It would be a mistake to insist that because America's policy toward Russia accomplished little, Churchill's own would have been effective. He scored a limited success in Greece and might have done more; but whether he could have entirely controlled the situation must be doubtful. In the matter of Poland, on which he and Roosevelt were fully agreed, they found themselves helpless and might very probably have done so whatever their methods. The most that can be claimed for Churchill's policy toward Russia is realism. One may also add that in his aspirations for postwar Europe, he appears generous and full of old-fashioned regard for Britain's obligations.

The history of Poland both during and after the war is among the most tragic in Europe. It was Poland who had first resisted Hitler, relying on the promised aid of England and France. Accordingly, in the lovely, unseasonable weather of September and October, 1939, the Poles had been exposed to the full force of the German Blitzkrieg operating under almost ideal conditions. Polish resistance had been gallant but utterly hopeless. When this was evident, the Russians had invaded Poland from the back and seized about half of the country. When therefore Germany attacked Russia in the summer of 1941, one could hardly have blamed the Poles if they had fought some on one side, some on the other, some for neither. To their great credit, they kept their heads and rallied round the Polish government which had been formed in London. In their usual grudging fashion, the Russians allowed certain Poles to enlist a Polish legion from the Russian prisoner-of-war camps. This was eventually allowed to depart for the Middle East, together with its horde of dependent women and children. However, a very large contingent of Polish officers known to have been in three prison camps close together had vanished without trace. These were not professional soldiers, but drafted men of the educated classes, the very flower in fact of Polish manhood. They were not found until April, 1943, when the Germans, who were by now in possession of the ground, published the discovery of their mass graves in the forest of Katyn.

The question now arose, who had massacred these people? Russians and Germans had both occupied the place for about a year. The reputation of neither made it unlikely. Each accused the other. Neither would allow an impartial investigation. Both were liars whenever their interest was served by lies. Weighing such evidence as there was, the Polish government came to the conclusion that the Russians had done this deed. It was too much. Giving way to natural feelings, the Poles in London broke off their relations with Russia. Churchill sympathized with them, as anybody with generous instincts would be bound to do; but he warned them that they were harming their own cause. They were not, however, for the moment to be persuaded.

Thus matters stood at the time of Teheran. His obliga-

tion to Poland was much on Churchill's mind, while
Roosevelt was conscious of the fairly large U.S. Polish
population. Thus both of them took up the question of
Poland with Stalin and for the moment appeared to reach
some accord. Stalin insisted on large parts of Poland for
Russia. He was not, however, unwilling to move Poland
west, giving her compensation out of Eastern Germany.
Considering the desert that Hitler had made out of Eastern
Europe by war, extermination camps, or enslavement, no
one had much sympathy for the German point of view.
Let them move their population.

Agreement in principle was shortly reached along these
lines, but when Churchill brought up the further question
of Polish-Russian relations, it became clear that trouble was
brewing. The Polish government in exile had played into
Stalin's hands. By now the Russians had set up a Polish
government of their own, having plenty of people still in
their power who could be persuaded to co-operate willy-
nilly. Stalin claimed this represented the true wishes of
the Polish people far better than the reactionaries and
traitors gathered in London.

It still seemed possible that through patient persistence
an accord could be worked out. Roosevelt and Churchill
continued to press the claim of the London Poles, while
Russian forces advanced to "liberate" the country. Churchill now found himself in the same position as at the beginning of the war. British troops were not in Poland. They
were not even in Austria and Hungary, as he would have
liked to see them. There really was nothing he could do
save put moral pressure on Stalin by telegram. He did his

utmost. Meanwhile, the Poles by an act of desperate gallantry sealed their own fate. Unsupplied, incompletely armed, the Polish Underground rose against the retreating Germans in Warsaw.

They rose relying on the Russian advance. The Russians, however, had no use for individualists in Poland. They had Polish leaders of their own who would do what they were told. The Russian army halted in its tracks to let the Germans put down Warsaw. American forces, who had offered to fly in supplies, were refused permission to land behind Russian lines and refuel to get back to their bases. The Warsaw radio was heard all over Europe appealing desperately for aid, until at last it died away.

With it must have died most of Churchill's hopes, not only for a free Poland, but for the future as a whole of Eastern Europe. The diplomatist, however, may not admit a defeat. It is always his object to get the best bargain he can. With tireless persistence, Churchill took up the cause of the Poles from a new position. Would it not be possible to get the London Poles and the Lublin Poles (as the pro-Russian group were called) to reach an agreement?

The Polish question was being aggravated by similar problems over Bulgaria and Rumania, who had already come under Russian occupation. It proved impossible to reach any understanding with Stalin by correspondence. The whole future of postwar Europe hung in the balance, and with it the future of the world. Meanwhile, the Allied armies in east and west stood on the very borders of German soil. The jubilant peoples of America and Great Britain saw the long task as nearly done. It was in a mood of outward rejoicing, but of deep anxiety and restlessness before coming change that Churchill prepared himself for his last great conference with Roosevelt and Stalin at the Russian Black Sea winter resort of Yalta.

He had a shock at the very outset. Roosevelt's appearance was terribly altered for the worse. The extraordinary personal charm of the President still remained, but no one could see him without wondering whether he could last the conference out. Fatigue was forcing him to delegate more and more. The general direction of American policy was slipping from his hands at the precise moment when Churchill wished to arouse him to vigilance. Nor was this all. Roosevelt opened the plenary meetings with a new statement of the American view. The war would soon be over, and America had not the slightest desire to dominate Europe. She wished above all to get out, and she could not in any case guarantee to supply occupation troops for more than two years. It was therefore necessary for an international authority to be set up at once in order to take over such problems as might remain. It was in this spirit that he urged on the conference the general proposals for a United Nations authority which had been drawn up at Dumbarton Oaks.

Stalin may have grinned at this. Churchill was certainly dismayed. He had not personally taken part in the discussions which had shaped the United Nations constitution. He had approved them; but embattled England, overcrowded already with American troops, menaced by buzz bombs, had hardly seemed the place for a long and leisured conference. Nor had he the time for such a thing.

On the bank of the Rhine. Churchill with Eisenhower, March, 1945.

The Supreme Moment. V-E Day, May 8, 1945.

A splendid uniform. The Lord Warden of the Cinque Ports
minus one epaulette, August, 1946.

Electioneering. Churchill supports a party candidate, February, 1949.

With friend and dog. Churchill walks with Bernard Baruch
in the grounds of Chartwell, July, 1949.

A green old age. Churchill arrives in America with Mrs. Churchill,
his daughter, Mary, and her husband, Christopher Soames, March, 1949.

Britain's highest honor. Churchill walks in procession to St. George's Chapel, where he will receive the Order of the Garter, June, 1954.

Famous Victory sign. In Washington, 1954.

Churchill bows out. Sir Winston and Lady Churchill receive Queen Elizabeth
to dinner the night before he retires from office, April 5, 1955.

Pomp and pageantry. Churchill inspects an honor guard of pikemen outside
the Guildhall, where a statue of himself is to be unveiled, June, 1955.

Eighty-five today. Churchill on his way to pay a birthday
visit to the House of Commons, November, 1959.

A British delegation had attended, naturally. General outlines had been approved, but there had been a deadlock with the Russians over the votes of the Security Council.

The conference at Yalta was the natural place to work out an agreement. This need not, however, have been linked to the American statement that two years was all they would give to policing Europe. The Russians certainly were planning a longer occupation. Britain alone did not possess the power to oppose Russia on a line drawn down the middle of Germany. There remained France with her long memory and her traditional fear of German aggression. Yet what was France but a scarecrow stuffed with straw? The American statement might well induce the Russians to give way on the United Nations in the hope of getting America out of Europe. As a contribution, however, to the future peace of the world, it could have but a negative value.

In spite of, or possibly because of this bad start, the Yalta Conference went unexpectedly well. A compromise which seemed reasonable was worked out, and the United Nations was set on its way to its first inauguration. There appeared evidence that the Russians actually desired to make it work. In the matter of Poland, they showed themselves harder to reason with, but finally agreed that the Lublin government should be enlarged to include representatives from London and also from occupied Poland. The new government should then be recognized by the Allies and should proceed to hold free elections. American and British observers should have access to see what was going on.

These great achievements took up the time of the conference — on the top level that is, for the size of the delegations ran into the hundreds, and many minor discussions on military and political affairs went on at once. Accommodations were at a premium in the war-torn town. Some of the British delegation were sleeping six to a room, and in the nineteenth-century palace provided for Churchill and his high brass, important people with their shaving tackle queued up for the three washbasins which were all that nineteenth-century habits had demanded. Hospitality, however, flowed as usual, and the efforts of the Russians to gratify their guests were fantastic. Notwithstanding, when Stalin accepted Churchill's invitation to dine, Russian police arrived, turned all the servants out of the reception rooms, and searched every square inch. Stalin appeared with a further armed guard of two dozen. Roosevelt was protected on the five-mile drive to Churchill's palace by an escort of policemen. Churchill was followed by two plainclothes detectives looking unobtrusive. All of these methods were just about equally effective, since nobody present had any motive for doing bodily harm. The Big Three themselves were jocular and friendly. They posed in the sun for a picture very popular at the time and very annoying to the Western World when it realized what troubles had lurked in the background. How dared Roosevelt in particular look so jaunty? It is difficult to see what else Roosevelt or Churchill could have done. The long association between the Big Three was producing certain results. They found it possible at this top level to hammer out agreements which the Russians seemed to accept. One could but trust them.

Within a month, it was perfectly clear that trust was misplaced. The Polish agreement was not worth the paper it was written on. The Lublin government was not enlarged. No Poles from London were allowed inside the country. Sixteen leaders of the Polish Underground were asked to a meeting with a promise of safe conduct — and there arrested and carried off to Russia. American and British observers were not permitted, lest they see what Russia was doing inside the country.

Churchill bestirred himself. He knew it was really urgent to act before the liberal and democratic groups were destroyed and spirits cowed. Yet without Roosevelt's strong support, he was not in a position to tackle Stalin firmly. This support he found he could not obtain. Actually, Roosevelt was no longer even drafting the telegrams signed in his name. He took few decisions by now, yet nobody else could make a bold step without him. American policy was marking time as men waited for the President to die. Thus the situation in Poland drifted from bad to worse. The iron curtain, which Churchill himself was the first to describe as such, came down on Europe.

The news of Roosevelt's death was a terrible shock. After Yalta, it had been perfectly clear Roosevelt was not well. However, the actual details of his condition had been concealed, so that no matter what Churchill surmised, he had never been certain that his correspondent was no longer really the President. The facts of the position burst on

Churchill suddenly now. His own and England's friend was dead. The new President, Mr. Truman, was a very dark horse. Churchill had never met him. Nobody in England knew him well. It had been his function to stand ready to take over, yet Roosevelt never acquainted him with what was going on. It stood to reason Truman could not take any firm stand for months to come, and what he would do then could only be guessed at.

Such considerations of statesmanship or patriotism formed merely part of a sorrow which was genuinely deep and personal. Churchill really loved the President. He was susceptible to Roosevelt's charm, admired the gallantry of his long fight against polio, and was personally grateful for many a gesture made for his sake, for many a piece of timely aid for England. Roosevelt and Marshall had been with him when he heard of the fall of Tobruk — one of the worst moments of the war. He had not forgotten their generosity then and the prompt dispatch of precious tanks to Egypt. He had written to Roosevelt on his sixtieth birthday, and Roosevelt had answered, "It's fun to be in the same decade with you." He had not forgotten that either. Above all, the two statesmen had fought for the same sort of world, and both had known it. Thus personal and political loss were hopelessly mixed. Churchill rang the bell for his detective, Thompson, who was asleep. He told him the news, tears rolling down his cheeks. He had not wanted company when the *Prince of Wales* was lost; but this was a more personal blow. Unselfconscious as ever, he turned to the nearest friend to share his sorrow.

Churchill was not the only leader in whom the President's death aroused profound emotion. Hitler and Goebbels with almost hysterical joy assured each other that a miracle had taken place. At the last moment Germany was saved, even as Prussia had been saved two centuries ago by the death of Catherine the Great. History, however, was not to repeat itself so tamely. Three weeks later, both Hitler and Goebbels were dead. In yet another week, when the negotiations for German surrender were complete, all fighting stopped. VE-Day dawned on May 8th, just five years to the day since Chamberlain had walked from an embittered House to shouts of "Resign, resign!"

VE-Day was most especially Churchill's. To no man in the world did that victory owe so much, and to no people did it mean more than to the English. Crowds had been gathering in the streets since the night before. Lights had blazed after long blackout. Somehow or other, in spite of shortages, silly things had appeared from nowhere — paper hats, false noses, buzzers, confetti, firecrackers even. People swung singing through the streets arm in arm, shoved at each other and laughed. St. Paul's and Westminster Abbey were packed for thanksgiving. Crowds were gathering outside the Palace and in Parliament Square. That morning Winston Churchill rode out of 10 Downing Street to make his official announcement to Parliament. It took him half an hour to drive a quarter of a mile. In fact, he did not drive, but was pushed along by people who wanted to pat his car, or just to see him, just to shout out, "Good old Winnie!" — just to feel that on this occasion in some direct, uncomplicated way they had thanked him. Crowds cheered him from the House to Buckingham Palace and back home.

They stood outside in the street and cheered for hours until he came out on the balcony of Number Ten Annex and spoke. Thereafter they kept on calling him back, and like a prima donna in love with her audience, Winston kept on coming.

He loved it all. Winston was never a spoilsport. No uneasiness about the future prevented him from understanding the people's mood today. He ordered an open car for the next morning so that he could ride high with his feet on the back seat, and in this position he was cheered all through the West End as he made official calls on the embassies of Britain's principal allies. In the evening, after a meeting at Number Ten, he found the closed car waiting to take him up to the Annex. He would have none of it, and decided to walk. It proved impossible to get through the crowd in Whitehall. His attendants tried to put him between two cars in the hopes of making headway and of preventing him from being knocked down by the crowd pressing around him. Finally he clambered up on the rear bumper of the car ahead, whence with willing assistance he scrambled onto the roof, crawled forward on hands and knees, and seated himself on the front, legs dangling over the windshield. Slightly pink from the exertion, panting, a little rumpled, there he sat and beamed at the upturned sea of faces — the lion of England, the bulldog, John Bull himself in the midst of his own people.

It was typical of Winston Churchill that he could give himself over to the uncomplicated, rollicking mood of the public though he was conscious of the shadow of the future advancing down the sunlit road to meet them. In his message to Parliament, he had stressed the difficulties which lay ahead and called on the people not to relax their efforts. He had reached the conclusion that there would have to be a showdown between the Western Powers and Russia. He must persuade the Americans to hold on, not to send everything to the Far East yet, not to co-operate with the Russians till Hungary, Austria, Poland, Czechoslovakia, in fact Eastern Europe was treated in accord with the Atlantic Pact and the spirit of Yalta.

It was now in particular that Churchill wished the Americans had taken his advice about striking up from Italy to Vienna or Budapest. He also had vainly urged them in the last few weeks of the war to drive for Berlin. But though these opportunities had been lost, the tide of fortune had carried the Western Allies well over a hundred miles deeper into Germany than the boundaries of their projected zone. They had therefore a real bargaining counter if they chose not to honor their own obligations until and unless the Russians honored theirs. The next big conference was due at Potsdam in July, and Churchill bent his efforts to keeping the Americans on their present line and persuading them to be firm.

He failed, and for a number of reasons. The long hiatus in American leadership still persisted. Truman hardly knew his mind yet. The last constructive effort of Rooseveltian statesmanship had been Yalta, and to Yalta with its atmosphere of jovial good will the Americans clung. Besides, the war with Japan still persisted. Churchill was genuinely anxious that Britain should now take a major share in this, as her position in the Far East justified. He did not, however, regard the struggle as one of major importance compared to the future of Europe. The Americans did.

Thus Churchill argued in vain. His influence in American government circles was nothing like what it had been. His popularity with the public and the American press had never quite recovered from the trouble over Greece. Besides, a new factor was impressing itself on the American mind. For the first serious time since 1940, Churchill's own dominance of the English political scene was coming in question.

Immediately following the defeat of Germany, Churchill had consulted with the Labour Leaders, Attlee and Bevan, about the future of his all-party national government. It had been his own expressed wish that the arrangement should last until the defeat of Japan. Had anyone foreseen that this would come in less than three months, there need have been no difficulty. Since, however, the American estimate was for eighteen months and it seemed wiser to suppose that like most wars this would drag on longer, Attlee and Bevan were not inclined to agree. The national emergency was certainly over. There would be an effort to be made, but the question of defeat no longer arose. The present Parliament had been elected ten years before under the leadership of Stanley Baldwin and over the long-dead issue of the Italian invasion of Abyssinia. It was customary to suspend elections during a major war, but the nation could not be indefinitely governed by a body so out of touch with its current feelings. Bevan and Attlee came back with a counterproposal that there be a three months' deadline, at the end of which, war or no war, the election must take place.

Churchill refused this arrangement. He could not take a strong line with Stalin or run a war with a rope round his neck. He would rather have the election at once; and so it was arranged. A date in July was decided upon. In the meanwhile, his Labour opponents resigned from the government in order to give themselves a free hand. A Conservative government under Churchill was formed to carry on business for a few weeks during the summer.

Both parties now found themselves in a strange position. Their long truce had left them uncertain which way the British cat was likely to jump. On the one hand, Labour put forward a carefully considered plan of socialized medicine, increased old-age assistance, insurance benefits of various sorts, and educational reform. They calculated that the common man wanted to have achieved something besides bare victory. He would remember the unemployment after the First World War. He would be ready to vote for the party which promised security against such ills in the future. The Conservatives in their turn proposed reforms, but on a minor scale. Fundamentally, Churchill had exhausted his radical impulses in 1908, and he was too honest to propose a great deal of public spending at a moment when he thought it really unwise. Perhaps he was suffering from an occupational disease of eminent politicians which ruined Lloyd George, ruined Smuts, and many another. World problems had become so absorbing that he took too little account of domestic details. However this may be, the Conservative program put forward in 1945 was far less attractive to the anxious common man than that of Labour. Most Conservatives thought little of the contrast. Their enormous, their quite overwhelming asset was simply Churchill.

So the world thought. So Churchill himself thought, though now and again he had certain qualms. His position was awkward. Attlee and Bevan, having resigned from office, could devote their time to campaigning. Churchill still governed, and with a great number of temporary men, at a time of importance. He was seventy, and the long strain had left its mark. He was desperately tired. After Cabinet meetings underground that winter and spring, he had had to be carried up the stairs. Perhaps he was losing his grip on the nation, since the people had begun to relax after strain and he could not. He dared not warn them too explicitly about Russia, lest he ruin the Anglo-American unity on which their fate depended. He could not keep people's eyes on the international scene when men who had been absent three, four, or five years from their families were coming home.

All these things must have influenced the manner of Churchill's plunge into the political arena after so many years of power. One consideration, however, appears of particular weight. He was over seventy. It might seem probable that after the Japanese war he would resign. Was it likely that the British public would vote Conservative for the sake of the privilege of being governed by Churchill just long enough to pave the way for Eden? Somehow or other if Churchill was to command the vote, he must convince the voter that he had energy left to last for a long while.

People as it happened had expected a few massive speeches from Churchill in the grand manner. With horrified surprise, they saw him come bouncing out of his corner to lay about his opponents in the good old election spirit. His energy was not applauded. As Low, the cartoonist, pointed out, one's admiration of the Grand Old Statesman was merely interrupted by this sudden appearance of the Naughty Old Politician. Labour leaders who had been treasured colleagues of Churchill's own a few months back were not going to plunge the country into a red revolution. It was useless for Churchill to carry on as though they were. But Churchill had lost his temper and his sense of proportion. He would not be quiet. The Potsdam Conference had been scheduled to open a few days before the election results came out, since these were deferred to get the votes of the servicemen still abroad. Churchill planned therefore to take over Attlee with him so that no matter which way the election went, both leaders would be present. In the meanwhile, Professor Laski, a Labour supporter of great brilliance but little tact, announced that the Labour Party would not consider itself bound by the decisions which Attlee or Churchill might make at Potsdam without them.

Cabinet ministers are not in this way made answerable to a party machine. Most sensible people knew perfectly well that Attlee would never allow it and that Laski had been in trouble before because of his rash tongue. When Churchill chose to pretend that a Labour administration would be slave to a secret dictatorship, he convinced no one. People shrugged again at that Naughty Old Politician. It was really a good deal Churchill's own fault that in one meeting he was actually hit by a stone. This had undoubtedly happened to him before in the lively twenties. Then it had been an occupational hazard which a pugnacious, hard-hitting politician might ignore. Now one of his own people, among whom he had paraded short weeks since perched high in the back of a car, had thrown that stone to hurt him. He made nothing of it, but certainly now and then he had his qualms.

He still could not really believe he would lose the election. Such ingratitude on the part of the people seemed monstrous. Besides, there was work to be done — unfortunately more important than the common man could be allowed to know. He could not put himself in the place of the voter who was choosing between the security he wanted and the figure of the grand old man who must be tottering more or less on the edge of retirement. Thus when the figures came in — a Labour landslide — Churchill was aghast. It felt indeed like being stoned, and for the rest of his life he never entirely got over his sense of betrayal. He recovered his humor in time. He even learned to accept the nation's gratitude. Yet three years after the event he wrote a paragraph whose bluntness gives a glimpse of his deep feelings: "Thus, then, on the night of the tenth of May, at the outset of this mighty battle, I acquired the chief power in the State, which henceforth I wielded in ever-growing measure for five years and three months of world war, at the end of which time, all our enemies having surrendered unconditionally or being about to do so, I was immediately dismissed by the British electorate from all further conduct of their affairs." [1]

---

[1] *The Gathering Storm.* Boston: Houghton Mifflin Co.

The 1945 ELECTION left bitter feelings, and not only in Churchill. Half the nation was anxious to dissociate itself from the ingratitude of the other half. Letters of sympathy, floods of presents both lavish and humble poured in on the grand old man. Nor were these demonstrations confined to Conservatives. Victorious Labour especially desired to be gracious. Churchill's service to the nation was above party politics. What reward did he want?

Short of victory at the polls, he could have had anything. He could, if he desired it, have had a dukedom and founded a house to rival Marlborough's. But why should he of all men covet an honor which would prevent his son and his son's son from ever leading the House of Commons? Why should he quit the Commons himself? How could he, knowing the dangers ahead, desert his country's cause? To the astonishment of almost everybody, Churchill announced he would not retire. He intended to remain fully active and to lead the Opposition.

Baffled, the government offered through the King the highest and simplest of the honors in royalty's power to bestow. The Order of the Garter, founded in the thirteenth century, has always been reserved for the first in the land. This time, however, it came through the hands of Labour, and Churchill refused it. The most that he would accept was the Order of Merit, a modern but distinguished creation with twenty-four living members whose selection is non-political. Earl Alexander, Earl Montgomery, and a host of other new peers soon joined the Lords. Mr. Churchill alone of England's great men went unrewarded.

At least he had not retired in anger or turned his back on his country's need. Nevertheless his feelings were grim. It was Attlee who announced the victory on VJ-Day. Churchill, driving unrecognized through the London streets in his closed car, looked out on the jubilant people in silence.

All the details of changing back to unofficial life proved very bitter. The process of moving from Chequers and 10 Downing Street was hard in itself. The loss of six private secretaries at a swoop was still more serious. Throughout the war years, Churchill's establishment had grown more complex by degrees; and he was too old now to simplify it. Before the war he had been moderately wealthy. Indeed, he was still so; but the value of the pound had greatly declined while income tax soared. His highly paid writing had been since 1939 cut off. To be sure, there is a pension for ex-Prime Ministers, but this looked ridiculous beside the cost of Chartwell or of Churchill's staff. For his duties in Parliament, he also needed a house in town.

There remained his greatest asset, the immense potential value of his war memoirs, should he ever be able at his age and while still active in politics to wade through the vast bundles, the veritable truckloads of documents that would be required. Ironically, his chief reward for saving his country lay in this ability to earn enormous sums

— subject always to surtax and income tax amounting to ninety-five per cent.

Gradually the strangeness of his new situation wore off. Old habits of life were resumed, old pleasures enjoyed, and mellower feelings took the place of anger. It was a refreshment to call Chartwell home again, to superintend damp and muddy exertions in which he no longer partook, to have his special cat there and his own dog, to restock the pond with goldfish, breed a few pigs, receive a present of black swans from Australia, and worry about foxes. He fell into some of the routines of old age, the gentle amble round the place in the afternoon, the refreshing nap now lengthened to two hours. He liked to think of himself as a Kentish man, his birthplace at Blenheim in Oxfordshire seeming far away. Perhaps of all functions he performed in his seventies, he enjoyed that of Lord Warden of the Cinque Ports the most. Before the discovery of the New World, there had been centuries when the five southern English ports facing France had been all-important. Their Lord Warden's duties were mainly ceremonial now, but their connection with English history and with the soil of Kent gave them particular value in Churchill's eyes. Besides, one must admit that the uniform was even more resplendent than that of Elder Brother of Trinity House — and it was also vaguely naval. Churchill still indulged himself in his little foibles without apology and quite simply because he enjoyed them. He took to flying the Lord Warden's special flag on the hood of his car and had it hoisted at Chartwell as a sign he was in residence.

Holidays were a renewed pleasure, not the occasional day

at Marrakesh or the convalescence from illness brought about by overexertion. He could go off to the south of France or to Italy for several weeks at a time and paint. Much as he loved the English countryside, he seldom painted it. The colors were too muted for his gay palette. Instead, he developed a system of bringing home half-finished paintings from abroad, together with photographs and picture postcards — anything to remind him of details which he would work on at leisure. His output of pictures, like that of words, was terrific; yet there was never an air of haste or carelessness about his work. Quite the contrary, he would take infinite pains to satisfy himself. He submitted pictures to the Royal Academy and was regularly hung, not as a curiosity, but as a painter who might not be of the very first class, but had an individual, bold style of his own.

All this slowing down, this greatly renewed pleasure in the recreations of his earlier life may have saved Churchill to play an important part once more. His health improved, and as opportunity served, he demonstrated how he could still rise to an occasion. Even his sense of humor reappeared. Someone suggested that he should make a tour of the cities of England so that they could do him honor. His reply dismissed the subject with: "I refuse to be exhibited like a prize bull whose chief attraction is its past prowess." Yet his life was not all holiday. He seriously had undertaken the production of his memoirs of the Second World War, which was eventually to run to a million and a half words. The actual labor of dictation and revision was vast, and yet this in itself was nothing to the task of assimilating the material. In his usual fashion, Churchill assembled a team for the purpose — secretaries, historians, technical experts, research workers, editorial assistants. As a distinguished reviewer put it, they "rolled forward through forests and prairies of wartime documents like a large reaping and binding machine, rejecting, codifying, and sorting." Yet ultimately this staggering quantity of material had to pass through a single mind and be reduced to shape there. To be sure, he had been the chief actor himself, yet he had worked under such pressure and the whole field of war had been so enormous that even his phenomenal memory could have only retained broad outlines heavily encumbered by a haphazard clutter of details. His final production is not quite as well written as his history of the First World War, but the intellectual effort involved is incomparably greater, as is the authority of the whole. For not as literature, nor even as history, but as the commentary of a great man on his own achievement it is unique, ranking only — to compare great things with small — with the *Commentarii de bello Gallico* of Julius Ceasar.

His financial reward was proportionately enormous. The only problem, after all expenses were paid, was to save anything from the hands of the tax collector. It was partly with this in mind that Churchill acquired a new hobby and a new business expense — a racing stable. He had always loved horses and riding. Polo by this time was long over for him, but in his seventies he still turned out for an occasional hunt. The racing stable, however, was a new sort of venture altogether. He treated it partly as a business with the details of which he wanted little to do, and partly as a whole series of new pets. He used to call up every morning to find out how his horses did, and on one occasion when an epidemic of coughing was reported, he bounded out of bed and rushed over before shaving to be sure that everything was being done for their comfort. He liked to win, though his bets were exceedingly modest. Very happily, he had considerable luck, especially with Colonist II, who won at Ascot and earned a very impressive total of prize money. His success if anything increased his popularity with the public, which was still anxious to gratify him with whatever he set his heart on. Good old Winnie leading in his winning horse got the special ovation which the people gave every time they saw he felt pleasure.

All these pursuits would have been far more than enough for the seventies of any normal man, and yet among them the chief business of life went on. He attended Parliament, held weekly luncheons for the heads of the Conservative Party, thrashed out with them all questions of tactics, both for the present and with an eye to the next election. And with a steady, disillusioned gaze he watched clouds gather in the international skies while he waited for the moment when it would be best to speak out.

He chose to do so in America, where his reputation was still higher than any living statesman's. Here he was not, as in England, merely the head of the party out of power. Besides, since 1944 policy had been made in America. Churchill went over in March, 1946, to accept an honorary degree at Westminster College, Fulton, Missouri, and to deliver a speech there under the chairmanship of President Truman. The occasion was just right, unofficial, and yet

lent importance by Truman's presence. The speech Churchill made is still remembered as the start of a new era.

In 1946, America was still glowing with the memories of
Yalta, European victory, and comradeship with Russia.
Foreign policy followed the line Roosevelt had laid down,
and the real position of affairs in Eastern Europe was
little understood. In fact, America cared only to get out of
Europe and bring all the boys home. In Britain, meanwhile, the socialist government felt special ties of friendship with Communists, with whom they were apt to assume their differences were minor. It was therefore with a
considerable sense of shock that people in both countries
heard Churchill speak out plainly in the old, ringing style.
"From Stettin in the Baltic to Trieste in the Adriatic, an
iron curtain has descended across the Continent." He even
compared these times with those of the thirties when he
had seen war coming and had warned in vain. If the
Western Powers would not call a definite halt to Russian
expansion, France, Italy, and the whole of Europe might
fall to the Communists, who were pursuing infiltration
tactics everywhere. And if it did so, the consequence to the
Atlantic powers would be disastrous.

The reaction of the English-speaking powers was peculiar. Almost unanimously the presses of both countries
raised an outcry. That old Russian-hater, that warmonger,
Churchill, was stirring up trouble again. It was all that
he ever had known how to do. Yet when these angry
noises died down to mutterings, it was seen that Churchill's
position in his country and the world was subtly altered.
Instead of being the obstinate old man who would not

retire, he had come forward once again as a leader and a statesman. The truth was, many were uneasy and had obstinately been trying to overlook unpleasant facts. In addition, the reaction of the hard-pressed democracies of Europe to Churchill's outspoken tirade was very different from that of America and England. When he spoke again a few months later in Zurich, he was received there with solid approval. Meanwhile, the phrase "iron curtain" had passed into the English language, and by this very fact had drawn attention to all the evidence which had been so hopefully overlooked. Thus, when the showdown between the free and the Communist worlds actually came with the Berlin airlift and the Korean War, the general outlook in America and England had been changing for some time. With disillusionment came swift reaction. Roosevelt perhaps was blamed too much. Now, it seemed to be Churchill who had been always right.

The General Election of 1950 was the moment when this growing change of view was put to the test in England. Churchill had learned his lesson. His campaign was far more sober in its treatment of the Socialists than last time. The Conservative Party had learned its lesson, too. Its younger leaders had produced a judicious program of reform to rival Labour's. According to rumor, the old man took little interest in this. He merely tolerated it as a means of satisfying people. Tory Democracy was lost to his view in the muddle of unfinished business which the war and the end of the war had left behind them.

The results of the 1950 election startled even the would-be prophets. Labour's majority, which had in 1945 been enormous, was cut to six. The Conservative comeback was a personal triumph for Churchill. It did not naturally make him Prime Minister yet; but it settled the question of whether he would become so. It was obvious that Labour could not last very long, and equally certain that the people wanted Churchill, not Eden as their leader. Eighteen months later at seventy-seven, Churchill came back with the tide. This time, however, he was not just the man for an emergency. He was the leader of a great party and accepted through good or bad. After half a century spent in Parliament, he had finally conquered not merely the hearts of the people, but their prejudice. He was trusted. His judgment, so often doubted before, was at last supreme.

He was difficult, of course — increasingly so — and much indulged. He did even more of his work in bed, in fact he never got up before lunch if it could be avoided. For this, however, he was invariably late, with luck ten minutes, but very frequently an hour. Other people's convenience waited unashamedly on his. In the Houses of Parliament, a bedroom was fitted up for him to undress and take his nap there between luncheon and the serious business of the afternoon session. His night hours, meanwhile, were as bad as ever before and without the excuse of the war emergency. He was growing deaf, and like many older people he heard with an effort that he did not care to sustain when he was bored. His hearing aid mainly annoyed him. Temperamental as ever, Churchill never had the least idea how to manage a machine. He learned, however, to fiddle with it during debates in order to enrage the Opposition.

In spite of these idiosyncracies, his business was done and well done. By a combination of good judgment and luck, he had his Indian summer after all. During his last prime ministership, the Korean War was brought to an end and the NATO organization built up. Clouds still menaced the world horizon, but in a less threatening way. For a moment after the armistice in Indochina in 1954, there was less open conflict in the world than at any time for forty years. The British economic position, which had been difficult after the war, was beginning to recover under Conservative care. Nor were relations between America and England neglected. One of Churchill's first acts as Prime Minister had been to plan and carry out an American tour.

Thus his era came to an end under a little patch of blue sky. The death of King George VI caused Churchill deep personal sorrow, but the accession of a young queen was still a symbol of transient gaiety. When the old man was offered the Order of the Garter once more, he accepted it, taking his place with the aristocracy of England as one who needed no title other than that of plain Sir.

With his sense of history, Churchill could see himself now on the highest pinnacle to which the Queen's subject could aspire. He had equaled Marlborough. And if he had not left a palace glowing with the tapestries of his great campaigns, yet he had left a record of them on the shelves of far more people than had ever seen the state of Marlborough. In his youth, men had accused Churchill of being too eager for personal glory because he had aspired to reach the top. They had called him "young man in a hurry." Yet now that he was at the top and had won the glory, he had learned to think in terms of being serviceable.

His long life was nearly spent. So many of the problems of the new welfare state and the new British Empire were not Churchill's sort of problem at all. He had spent his last energies on unfinished business of his own, the constant strengthening of the Anglo-American alliance of which he had been the chief architect, and the problem of Russia. It was time to turn over British affairs into other hands and retire. Soon afterwards he had a stroke, and then another. Lady Churchill, ten years younger than he, sustained him now; while secretaries fended off the public. He declined very slowly, took his holidays, paid a visit to Eisenhower in the White House, and toured Greece. In the 1959 election, he made a campaign speech — and everybody agreed a surprisingly good one. He still met people to a limited extent, and they confided behind their hands to friends that he was shockingly old. The papers published a kindly photograph now and then, but for the rest held their peace.

Churchill was already lapsing into legend. Everybody who had known him rushed out a book — and the public devoured them all. There seemed no limit to people's desire to get to know him, nourished no longer by his own speeches and words, but by every trivial detail from his white silk underwear to the temperature of his bedroom or the patent spit-collectors he sometimes used to use with his cigars. No man ever had come under such a microscope, been bathed in such a glare. The love of a people for a man takes on strange forms, and very luckily this one caused Churchill no concern. His privacy was not disturbed thereby, for he had never been personally self-conscious, nor had he needed to strive in any way to be unique.

Index

166, 206–10; Newfoundland meeting with Roosevelt, 168–69; trip to U.S. after Pearl Harbor, 177–81, 182, 183–84; flies across Atlantic, 184–85; blamed for British reverses, 185–86, 194–96; methods of speech-writing and work, 186–89; answers criticism with speech, 189; given vote of confidence, 190; makes ministerial changes, 191; and responsibility for Singapore, 192; and problem of India, 193; in U.S. again, 200–203; motion of censure against fails, 203; appearance at age sixty-eight, 211; at Casablanca, 211, 212; and strategy in Mediterranean, 214; ill in North Africa, 216; trip to Washington, 216–17; and plans for cross-Channel attack, 218; opposed to war in China, 218, 219; and Chiang Kai-shek, 219, 222–23; asks Roosevelt for landing craft, 220, 221; at Teheran, 225–28; ill in Tunis, 228; and preparations for cross-Channel invasion, 230–34; views on postwar Europe, 238–39; waning popularity in U.S., 239, 241, 254; and the Greek crisis, 239–41; and Polish problem, 243, 244; at Yalta, 246, 248; and Roosevelt's death, 249–50; on VE-Day, 251–52; and 1945 elections, 255–59; as opposition leader, 260; refuses Order of Garter, 260; accepts Order of Merit, 261; changes to unofficial life, 261–65; holidays, 262–63; undertakes memoirs of Second World War, 263–64; acquires racing stable, 264; iron curtain speech at Fulton, Mo., 265–66; Prime Minister again, 268–69; accepts Order of the Garter, 269; declining years, 270–71

Ciano, Count, 143

Cinque Ports, Churchill made Lord Warden of, 262

Coal strikes, Welsh, 42–43, 92–93

Collier's Magazine, 100

Collins, Michael, 83

Colonist II, racehorse, 265

Committee for Air Defence Research, 108

Committee of Imperial Defence, 44, 73

Communist parties, 237–38

Congress, Churchill invited to address, 179

Conservative Party, 11, 13; Churchill annoys, 38, 39, 75–76; demand Churchill's dismissal from Admiralty, 68; Churchill rejoins, 89; 1945 program, 255–56; makes comeback, 267–68

Constantinople, 84

Cooper, Alfred Duff, 128

Coral Sea, Battle of, 194

Coronel, disaster at, 53

Cradock, Admiral, 53

Cripps, Sir Stafford, 191

Cuba, Churchill in, 21

Cyprus, Churchill at, 214, 216

Czechoslovakia, crisis in, 114–19

Damascus, seizure of, 80

Damaskinos, Archbishop, 241

Dardanelles, Churchill's plan to open, 62–65; internationalized, 84; Churchill's defense of actions concerning, 88

de Gaulle, General Charles. See Gaulle

De Roebeck, Admiral, 66

Desert, war in, 185, 201–2. See also Auchinleck, Desert Army, Egypt, North Africa and Rommel

Desert Army, 196, 202, 205, 206

Dill, Field Marshal Sir John, 178, 181

Disraeli, Benjamin, 11, 12, 14

Duchy of Lancaster, Churchill as Chancellor of, 69, 74

Duke of York, H.M.S., 178, 184

Dundee, 85

Dunkirk, Germans threaten (World War I), 55; defenses improved, 137–38; evacuation of, 139–40

"Dunkirk Circus," 55

Durban, 22

East Indies, loss of, 181, 192
Eden, Sir Anthony, 114, 268
Edward VIII, abdication of, 109–10
Egypt, army reinforced in, 143; Churchill eager to get more troops into, 173; war in, 146, 202, 203–4; Churchill wants to visit, 203, 205; Churchill in, 206, 214, 216, 222
Eighth Army, British, 210, 211
Eisenhower, Dwight D., 228, 233, 270
Elections, general, of 1945, 254–59; of 1950, 267–68; of 1959, 270
Elizabeth II, accession of, 269
Emden, ship, 52, 53
Estcourt, defense of, 22–23
Eugénie, Empress, 3, 6

Far East, war in, 167, 173–77, 181–82, 191–94
Feisal, Emir, 80, 81
Finland, 126, 162, 236
Fisher, Admiral John, 47, 59; negative to Dardanelles plan, 66–67; resignation, 68
France, and the Agadir crisis, 32; treaty with Czechoslovakia, 115; decides not to fight for Czechoslovakia, 116; attitudes on World War II, 124; defeat of, 134–36, 141–42; German submarine bases in, 158; plans for invasion of, 199–200, 204, 213, 221, 225; invasion takes place, 233; southern, plans for invasion of, 235
Free trade, doctrine of, 37–38
French Equatorial Africa, Bismarck demands, 34
Fulton, Mo., Churchill speech at, 265–66

Gallipoli expedition, 63–65, 69
Gamelin, General, 135–36
Gaulle, General Charles de, 212
George, David Lloyd. See Lloyd George, David

George VI, 111, 232, 269
German Imperial Fleet, 52–53
Germany, and the Agadir crisis, 32–36; treaty with Bolsheviks, 78. See also Hitler
Giraud, General Henri, 212
Gladstone, William, 11, 12
Gneisenau, ship, 52, 53, 195
"Goats," 13, 14
Goebbels, Joseph, 251
Goeben, ship, 52, 53
Gold standard, restoration of, 91
Gort, General, 136, 137
Gott, General W. H. E., 206
Graf Spee, ship, 126
Greece, attacked by Italy, 147; campaign in, 147–48; resistance of, 160, 213; King of, 237; Churchill defends British stand on, 239; crisis in, 240–41; Churchill tours, 270
Greenwood, Rt. Hon. Arthur, 120
Grenadier Guards, Churchill joins, 71
Grey, Lord, 56

Haiphong, bombardment of, 82
Halifax, Edward, Lord, 131
Hanfstaengl, Herr ("Putzi"), 102
Harbors, artificial, 144, 218
Harrow School, Churchill at, 14
Hitler, Adolf, Churchill sees as threat, 101–2; reoccupies Rhineland, 107–8; annexes Austria, 114; and Czech crisis, 114–17, 119; invades Poland, 120; invades Norway, 127; invades Holland and Belgium, 130; reluctant to fight U.S., 159, 160; turns main effort against Russia, 160–62; decides to fight for Tunisia, 213; death, 251
Holland, Hitler invades, 130
Hong Kong, siege of, 178
Hopkins, Harry, 168
Hozier, Clementine. See Churchill, Lady Clementine
Hyde Park, Churchill at, 201, 219

Iceland, Churchill in, 172

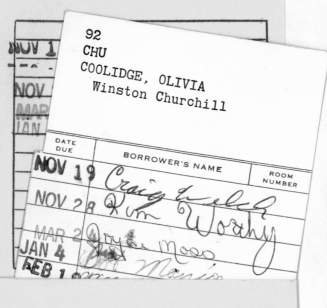